Designs for Fund-Raising

Designs for Fund-Raising

Harold J. Seymour

Second Edition

with introduction
by Charles E. Lawson

FRI FUND-RAISING INSTITUTE
a division of The Taft Group
12300 Twinbrook Parkway, Suite 450, Rockville, MD 20852

Library of Congress Catalog Card Number: 88-82007

Copyright © 1988 by the Fund-Raising Institute, a division of The Taft Group, 12300 Twinbrook Parkway, Suite 450, Rockville, MD 20852, 301-816-0210

ISBN 0-930807-07-3

To my wife, Martha Andrews Seymour

About the Author

$\mathcal{H}$arold J. Seymour, known to his professional friends as "Si," was a fund-raising executive and consultant in the earliest days of organized fund-raising. He was born in 1894, in St. Paul. In 1916, he was graduated from Harvard College and became a U.S. Navy aviator attached to the balloon service during World War I.

In 1919, fresh out of the Navy, he joined the staff of the Harvard Endowment Fund Campaign, which was the first large-scale attempt to raise money for higher education. That was the start of a 49-year career in fund-raising during which he gave counsel to Ivy League universities — including Barnard, Cornell, Princeton, University of Pennsylvania, and Yale — the YMCA, the Girl Scouts of America, the Salvation Army, the American Cancer Society, the United Negro College Fund, the Catholic Relief Services, the United Jewish Appeal, Johns Hopkins University, the Washington Cathedral, the Jewish Theological Seminary of America, and many others.

He was Executive Vice President of the John Price Jones Company, one of the field's earliest consulting firms.

During World War II, the American nation itself was his client. In 1941-42, he was fund-raising Campaign Manager for the USO. Then from 1942 to 1945 he was General Manager of the National War Fund. From offices in the Empire State Building, he conducted nationwide appeals — raising

$321 million to support 23 humanitarian, war-related agencies.

He guided the emergence of the new fund-raising profession as a founder and early president of the American Association of Fund-Raising Counsel.

And he died in 1968 at the age of 73.

Introduction

to the Second Edition

One might reasonably inquire why, after so many years, this book has been republished without one phrase altered — without any changes to reflect a ten-fold increase in giving and the technological advances that have so enhanced the capabilities of today's fund-raiser.

The reasons are clear and concise. First, the author captured the *essence* of both fund-raising and American philanthropy, i.e., volunteerism and personal involvement. Second, he had an *uncanny sense* of the universally applicable principles that leapfrog the decades. Third, Si Seymour wrote this book for fund-raising's "newcomers and trainees" for whom he had a special concern and a lasting message that transcends numbers, current practices, and the literature of his day.

When it appeared in 1966, *Designs for Fund-Raising* was the first major "how-to" book ever written about fund-raising. The author's vision was so broad, his foresight so strong, that even today this volume remains the most helpful and important book ever written on philanthropic fund-raising, its principles, patterns, and techniques. It is, in a word, *the classic* of the field — still the best source of basic insights and understanding a fund-raising executive can hope to find. True, some of the statistics and details have changed since 1966. (Those changes are marked by small numbers in the text and are annotated at the back of this volume.) But the insights and understanding remain as true and valuable as the day they were written, perhaps even more so.

This book is quoted more often in fund-raising circles than Benjamin Franklin is quoted in everyday life. It is referred to in an estimated *fourth* of all fund-raising literature that is published today.

Perhaps one reason it is quoted so often is shown in the recollection of a self-described "disciple of Seymour" who says, "The difference that distinguished Si Seymour from everyone else was his ability to take actual experience beyond the particular and into general principles that could be applied to all fund-raising experience."

Fortunately, Si Seymour's training under the tutelage of the noted John Price Jones coincided with the fund-raising profession's formative, definitive years and was a fertile source of experience and knowledge about this emerging field. Led by Seymour, the alumni of John Price Jones Company (now Brakeley, John Price Jones Inc.) produced more writing about fund-raising than any other organization in its time.

And Si Seymour had a singularly engaging way of giving his fund-raising advice. I can't help but repeat Si's irresistible comment that publicity about bequests "doesn't really matter very much, so long as you follow the law of the iceberg: some small part of it must have constant visibility."

One might easily misconstrue such jaunty stuff as lacking in substance (though time has proven the exact opposite to be true). In 1966, Ed Gemmel of Princeton University cautioned prospective readers against dismissing *Designs for Fund-Raising* lightly:

> The book is written so clearly and entertainingly that the reader may be seduced into zipping along briskly....[However].... I do *not* urge dipping into the Seymour book. I urge *wallowing* in it. The hippopotami on the Victoria Nile waddle in and submerge themselves until only their eyes, and I presume their eyebrows (I was too close to see exactly), float above the surface like two black tennis balls. *That's* the way to approach this book.

Si Seymour lived by his own philosophy that "business flourishes best in an atmosphere of joyous adventure." Partially, this was driven by his personal vendetta against pretentious, ponderous prose. "I think I'd still rather write as I've always tried to do," he explained, "instead of making the struggle to follow the prose style of the Ph.D. aspirants."

But largely, this philosophy grew from Si's irrepressible sense of humor. Whether in print or in person, Si Seymour imparted his knowledge in witty and wonderful ways. On the subject of causes led by notable, very important personages he wrote, "The first point is that there was nothing inside the shirts of these men but the men themselves." In person, he delivered such pearls of wisdom with considerable animation and aplomb. David Dunlop, director of capital projects at Cornell University, defines himself as "the number one fan of Si Seymour." He recalls:

> I came into the field in 1959, when Si Seymour was legendary. After the senior people on campus had completed their meetings with Si, they would assemble us young ones to meet with him. Si would drop one pearl of wisdom after another. I can remember him telling us, for example, how to begin an encounter with a volunteer leader. "Get yourself a good watch," he would say, loosening his own leather strap and dangling his timepiece before our neophyte eyes. Si was *showing* us to value a volunteer's time — not just *telling* us. He was like a motion picture — a teacher of the first order.

This quality also stemmed, in large measure, from Si's ability to make ideas both digestible and palatable: *digestible* because he frequently simplified concepts into bite-sized categories like "Fund-Raising's Two Mossiest Myths" or "The Seven Deadly Sins of Fund-Raising," coining a phrase whenever it would help convey a point; *palatable* because he created delectable ideas. He recommended against what he called "The Saturday Night Shave," or the once over lightly technique. "That's all right with a beard," he wrote, "but it is almost always fatal in a fund-raising campaign," hitting home, once again, the point that fund-raising is a personal business. How appropriate that *Designs for Fund-Raising* was originally published with the following comment on its jacket. It's from

Lyman S. Ford, former executive director of the United Community Funds and Councils of America:

> Si Seymour knows all there is to know about raising money for philanthropic purposes. When this is garnished by his great skill at transferring wisdom and experience into delightfully readable prose, the result is indeed a tasty morsel.

Even when Seymour's topic was solemnly serious, his words were vivid and visual. In his first book, *Design for Giving*, he described the formation of the National War Fund in World War II with a magnificent passage about "the circling ripples" of philanthropy which "became a rising tide."

"And even we native Middle Westerners know that a rising tide lifts all the boats," he added.

The result of all this was a wholly engaging man with a fine sense of humor — a man whose professional life was "a joyous adventure" and whose personal life was no less so.

When Si became irreversibly ill and was hospitalized, his humor was also incurable. One of his nurses reportedly told him that he sounded like Jimmy Stewart, to which Si replied, "I'm really the Duke of Windsor in disguise!"

Despite his demeanor of joviality, Si Seymour was taken seriously — to the degree that, although he was an Episcopalian, the Order of Knights of Sylvester was conferred upon him by the Roman Catholic Church under the instruction of Pope Paul VI. This award was made on Palm Sunday, three or fours days before he died, in recognition of his service to Catholic charities.

Si passed away on April 10, 1968, his wedding anniversary — married 48 years to the day — a poetic touch not unlike those contained in the words he said and wrote throughout his life.

The legacy of Si Seymour continues to be felt today, as fund-raising becomes an ever-greater force in American philanthropy. His great accomplishment was to elevate fund-raising above the level of common practice, helping to propel the circling ripples of philanthropy into a rising tide. And, as Si might have said, even *we* know that a rising tide lifts all the boats.

Now, see how Si himself describes this book in his preface to the first edition.

Charles E. Lawson
Chairman and CEO
Brakeley, John Price Jones Inc.

October 1988

Preface

𝒥elix Frankfurter said that the business of the United States is not business, it is civilization. And certain it is, from earliest times, that the good American has found it not enough to enrich his mind, earn a living, praise God, serve the state, raise a family, and have fun—that there has always been other work for him to do.

This other work has manned our voluntary agencies and has built our churches, schools, colleges, universities, museums, and all our other instruments of civilization. To be sure, government has had to move in when tasks such as these have outgrown voluntary action. But the private process has kept ever growing and spreading, with philanthropic giving now close to $11 billion a year, some thirty million volunteers listed as workers, and hundreds of thousands of agencies certified for tax-deductible gifts. [1]

Such a record, as Herbert Hoover pointed out on his ninetieth birthday, gives us many good reasons for national pride. But we tend to be more complacent about it than most of us have any right to be. The average American still gives less than 4 per cent of his taxable income, against the 30 per cent encouraged by Federal law.[2] Most of the significant giving by individuals is still done by the relatively poor, by the very rich of the second or third generation, and by those with a genuinely religious motivation, whose giving is therefore part of their way of life. And as for all those "workers," let us not delude ourselves—more of them merely lend their names than really bend their backs.

The point to be made, in the interest of moving our civilization forward at the desired rate, is that we could and should be doing a lot better. For it is surely clear now that in the decades ahead more causes, with more good reasons, will be seeking more funds from more people than ever before.

That, simply, is the main reason for this book. My purpose is to summarize what many good people have learned about fund-raising in the last fifty years or so, and to arrange the findings so that the essential processes can be better understood and better enjoyed, and become more fruitful. Accordingly, I hope to explain not merely what should be done, but when and why.

The people I hope to be talking to are not so much my old friends and colleagues, the old pros, as the newcomers and trainees, those who may be considering fund-raising as a career and those in the rising ranks of volunteers who either want to know more about the raising of money for their own guidance or satisfaction or wish to be able to explain things better to those they have to recruit or lead.

I believe that even the wisest of the old pros have trouble with perspective, that participation comes more readily when people know the background and the reasons for the tasks they are asked to assume, and that most of the troubles in organized fund-raising are due either to ignored or misunderstood laws and principles or to proceeding in the wrong order or at the wrong times.

Those beliefs explain the plan of this book, as outlined

in the Table of Contents, and explain too why my story begins and ends with people. Every cause, I hope to show, needs people more than money. For when the people are with you and are giving your cause their attention, interest, confidence, advocacy, and service, financial support should just about take care of itself. Whereas without them—in the right quality and quantity, in the right places, and the right states of mind and spirit—you might as well go and get lost. So you'd better know as much about people as you can, keep it ever in mind, and always let it light your way.

The vineyards of philanthropy are pleasant places, and I would hope many more good men and women will be drawn there. Most of all, I would hope it will be better understood that if these vineyards are to thrive and bear their best fruit, they must always have first-class attention.

Harold J. Seymour

Contents

Section *1*

Essential Background for Fund–Raising

What We Need to Know about People
The Makings of a Cause
Current Patterns for Gifts and Givers

Chapter 1

What We
Need to Know
about People

*I*n organized fund-raising, as indeed in any form of group persuasion, a good way to begin is to learn as much as you can about people. You need to understand, for instance, that genuine leadership in any cause is rare, beyond price, and always the nucleus of significant achievement. And you ought to know too that whatever your goals of persuasion may be and whatever your cause, there are three different kinds of people involved.

Knowing these distinctions and taking them into account is important in all sorts of promotion. In fund-raising, this will govern your planning and your timing, strongly affect your costs, and largely determine the eventual number of gifts and the amount of the dollars.

3

So first of all, I propose to discuss leaders and the three kinds of people. Next, I'll point out the two human aspirations that seem to matter most of all and then suggest which of the basic motivations can best move people to substantial action. After that, I shall review what all people *tend* to do—in directions important to organized persuasion. And finally, I shall remind you of the one ancient human fear that still gives the whole world the greatest trouble, and must therefore figure in all we say and do. Know these things and ponder on them, and you'll be well on your way.

In any field of human activity, not just in fund-raising, the leaders are indeed rare—never more than 5 per cent of any group or constituency, and usually less. These are the creative citizens, with what Harry Emerson Fosdick has called "a sense of privilege." They light the way, originate action, take the responsibility, establish the standards, create the confidence, sustain the mood, and keep things moving.

And then, about 25 or 30 per cent of the total, is the key group best described as *responsible*. For they are the ones who can be depended upon to play a thoughtful and proportionate part in any program engaging their advocacy and support. True, they need leadership and guidance, as everyone does, and are susceptible as all of us are to the climate and the planned action. But it is not for them that planners must provide supervision, system, and the goad. They will do what they say they will do and will try to do it the way you want it done. They are, obviously, simply wonderful.

Then come the merely *responsive,* that major group that will probably respond in varying degrees if all the portents and pressures are about right. They rarely act out of sheer impulse, unless negatively. The burdens of inertia and procrastination are ever with them. And while their hearts are warmed when their loyalties and compassions are stirred, they must always constitute the principal target for all the arts of organized persuasion, and all the best skills of the fund-raiser.

Finally, at the bottom and merging with the larger group noted above, is the inert fifth. This is the ultimate residuum, which exercises the rights and privileges of citizenship only under direct compulsion and daily shows us in the opinion polls that it can rarely even make up its mind about anything. The finest rhetoric never reaches these people, if only because they are not there to listen. Yet their lamentations never cease, and they are always the first to threaten to cut off the support they have hardly ever given. Well earned here would be the epitaph, "He could always be counted upon to be unreliable."

For any major type of campaign, some weird rule of three seems to be involved here, which should be heeded even though it is hard indeed to understand. For it has long been customary to say, at the upper levels of fund-raising, that a third of the money has to come from the top ten gifts, the next third from the next 100 gifts, and the last third from everybody else.[3] Similarly, with most of the workers in most campaigns, it is usual to say that a third will perform as asked (the responsible ones), a third group will respond under pressure and prodding, and the last third, no matter what you or anyone else does, will turn out to be mostly deadwood; there will just be time, if all goes well, to reassign their unfinished work to the performing top third, God bless 'em, who meanwhile will have finished their jobs.

So much for the three kinds of people, and their leaders. And now for other things we should know about them.

Two Universal Aspirations

It is pleasantly easy to say that everyone wants to be loved, admired, respected, remembered favorably, treated fairly, and never played down. But it has always seemed to me that we need something more specific than these usual generalities. And I think two top psychiatrists have shown the way.

Dr. Lawrence C. Kolb, my Tenafly neighbor, director of the New York State Institute of Psychiatry, and chairman of the department at Columbia, discussed these pages with me, and said he thought that what people want most is simply "to be sought." Millions today are hospitalized or under custodial care, he pointed out, for no better reason than because they think nobody wants them, cares about them, or wants to listen to what they have to say. The obverse of this, I think, should be obvious and highly significant.

Cornell's Dr. Dorothea C. Leighton, after a long study of underprivileged Indian tribes in Canada, concluded that every individual needs to feel that he is "a worthwhile member of a worthwhile group." And when you read that simple and wonderful phrase over a few times and reflect about it, you will begin to sense how fundamental it is and how universally applicable.

Certainly if your appeal misses these two universal aspirations, you'll miss many targets and have a much harder time. Play them well and consistently, and you'll go far.

Basic Motivations

It appears to be a logical corollary—assuming we all aspire to be sought and to be worthwhile members of worthwhile groups—that there can hardly be any stronger motivation for supporting a group or cause than simple *pride of association*. Certainly any feeling of indifference to an affiliation, worse yet any feeling of shame or hostility, and plain lack of confidence are about the most serious blocks to persuasion one could possibly imagine.

Obviously, pride needs a base of loyalty and favorable attitudes toward the institution, its activities, and its personnel. Pride can be and is nurtured by communication and ceremonials. But the one thing that triggers it into action better than anything else is actual participation in program. At a minimum, this involves consistent attendance at meaningful meetings and stated services. At best, it involves acceptance of real responsibility for committee work. And that is what leads most surely to advocacy and support. Those workrooms where the uniformed ladies have worked so well and so long have always been the real beef behind the support of the American Red Cross. Committee work is of the very essence of the Junior League, of boards, service clubs, alumni bodies, chest organizations, and any other activity notable for its good name and sound organization. Put pride together with involvement in program, and you have something literally beyond price.

The other basic motivation, I think, becoming more and more significant as any cause climbs the ladder from popular approval all the way up to action by its power structure, is *responsible concern for continuity.* McGeorge Bundy put it this way in his Phi Beta Kappa oration at Harvard in 1965: "to hold to one another across the generations." Most causes, I think you will find, prosper best in terms of keeping faith with the past, keeping step with the present, and keeping some real or implied promise to posterity.

What People Tend to Do

Abraham Lincoln, in that famous quotation about fooling the people, conceded, as we all should, our occasional gullibility. But he had unlimited confidence, as not many leaders do, in the ultimate popular wisdom.

Perhaps the one most important thing for persuaders to remember about people is never to play down to them but always to approach them with due respect for their idealism, courage, and intelligence, with full and open confidence in their response to bold leadership and challenging programs. Sir Winston Churchill noted this in one of his observations on the American people: "Their national psychology is such that the bigger the idea the more wholeheartedly and obstinately do they throw themselves into making it a success."

And now, here are some things people tend to do which should be of special interest in organization work:

To Follow Leaders Who Have Their Confidence. When the leadership is right and the time is right, the people can always be counted upon to follow—to the end and at all costs. Churchill alone, in the blackest hours of World War II, was proof enough of this. Conversely, Lincoln warned us, "If you once forfeit the confidence of your fellow citizens, you can never regain their respect and esteem." Confidence is the key here, for leaders, causes, and institutions alike. Lack of confidence, on the other hand, is a sure road to rejection.

To Strive for Measurable and Praiseworthy Attainment. All the admirable abstractions, such as virtue and probity, offer fine food for meditation and win ready endorsement. But let's not forget that what got many of us out for Sunday school was that series of pins for attendance. Just as football teams need goal lines, causes of all kinds need quota systems and measurable objectives, if you really want the people to get out there and play. There simply has to be a way to win, and a reason for cheers.

To Seek or Achieve Unity by Group Action. Many a cause has improved a faulty public posture merely by putting a lot of volunteers to work and thus multiplying its advocates. It is well to remember too these days that most of the parades for causes are not so much for the purpose of impressing those who watch as for unifying those who belong, and especially those who march.

To Act Only under the Pressure of Deadlines. One fact of life we usually find it convenient to ignore is that whatever we have plenty of time to do is often the thing that never gets done. It seems to be popular to decry pressure. Nobody likes the words, "Do it now," but on the other hand one of the greatest soporifics since Rip van Winkle is the line, "at your convenience." Whether the deadlines are genuine or merely plausible, there has to be a fairly imminent time limit on whatever you wish to persuade people to do.

To Relish Earned Reward and Recognition. Napoleon conceded that baubles won no wars, but it was Napoleon himself who founded the Legion of Honor. Those small fish fed to the trained seals every time they do a trick, the buttons and pins awarded for long service, the diplomas, certificates, and other evidences of personal involvement in worthwhile groups —all have a message here.

To Repeat Pleasurable Experiences, and Vice Versa. You hear many cries of "worker fatigue" in voluntary activities these days. But the usual trouble with volunteers is not killing them with overwork, but simply boring them to death. As with the arts of hospitality, the rule is that if they have a good enough time, they won't want to leave, and they'll be pretty sure to come back.

To Conceal Unpraiseworthy Attitudes. Here we have the reason for phony answers to opinion polls and the reason why so many join committees either out of fear of criticism by their peers or in perfunctory submission to social or business pressures—without in either case having the slightest intention of performing adequately by word, deed, and gift.

To Lose Our Sense of Community, with More Mobility and Greater Numbers. Now that the average American family moves every five years and there is coming to be greater variety in our proximity to new or different groups, all of us are probably tending to lose some of our sense of community. The results, all fund-raisers should note, are that many try to do by mail what we used to do by personal visitation and that some of the loyalties and competitive values of local appeals tend to get lost. And that's too bad, for when you stop to think about it, you will realize that all money has to be raised locally, where people are.

And now, here are some things all of us tend to do which should be of special interest in public relations and publicity work:

To Give Incomplete Attention and Indeed to Shorten the Attention Period Itself. At best, with few exceptions, people don't pay close or careful attention to anything. And short of war or national calamity, you can keep the people interested for just so long and then no longer. If the task is still unfinished when the time span is up, you have to reset the stage, shuffle the cast, change the words and music, and virtually start all over again. You can say, and rightly, that there is an exception in the field of religion. But even there the seasons and calendars recognize that even forty days is a long, long time.

To Glance Instead of Read. If they pay for it, they'll read it —maybe, and even probably. But in any works of organized persuasion, including fund-raising, it is doubtful that there has ever been a time when what E. B. White calls "the sweet uses of brevity" have been at such a premium. The shortening limits of attention periods and the tightening tensions in the costly and unremitting fight for the public eye and ear both tell us now that the safest thing is to convey the message almost phrase by phrase and leave it to repetition and the visual aids to pound the message home.

To Admire Excellence but to Suspect Perfection. The well-loved Pope John XXIII is said to have squirmed at the very mention of "infallibility," even within its two highly restricted meanings. And I like to remember too what Columbia's Professor Montague said to the YMCA's Eugene Barnett many years ago: "If you want to persuade anyone, you can't afford to be more than 85 per cent right." Certain it is that the very word "perfect," either as a verb or as an adjective, should be used sparingly if at all—except, perhaps, in purely theological discourse.

To Generalize from Acceptable Fragments. It may be lamentable, and further proof that even our best brains seldom function at more than 10 per cent of capacity, but it is nevertheless useful to know that most people, instead of thinking anything all the way through, prefer the short and easy jump to generalities. It takes very little to confirm a prejudice and not much more to rationalize a favorite opinion. So people tend to believe what their chosen leaders tell them and to be impressed by parables, testimonials, examples, categories, and all other short cuts in the arts of persuasion. And because they find it so much easier to assume that all samples truly represent the whole, we should always be careful with our samples.

To Respond to the Warmth of Good Sentiment. When Harvard's retired Prof. Howard Mumford Jones addressed his colleagues at a farewell dinner given by the English department, he said that the three most powerful words in any dialect are "justice, virtue, and love." Commenting further on the soul of a people and what it looks back to with pride and affection, he quoted Andrew Fletcher of Saltoun: "Give me the makings of the songs of a nation, and I care not who makes its laws." That is about all that needs to be said here, and it could hardly be said better. We simply need to remember that when you want the heart to prompt the mind to go where logic points the way, nothing can match the warmth of good sentiment.

To Prefer Incomplete Exposure—Even a Little Mystery. It has been plain enough for quite a while that diamonds win more girls than dishpans. And the lofty principle involved here should remind us never to go too far in confronting the people with all the mundane minutiae. By all means keep the posture of willingness to tell all, but leave a little room for dreams. Other things being equal, the people can always fashion in their own hearts a far better rationale for their support than any of us could ever devise from any long parade of facts and figures.

To Like a Due Amount of Dignity in the Images of Their Leaders. Smiles and laughter have their good place with our leaders, but never at the loss of basic dignity. Perhaps one of the reasons Calvin Coolidge chose not to run again was that awful picture of him in the headdress of a Sioux Indian chief. Charles de Gaulle, who has parlayed the dead pan into a very big thing indeed, puts it this way: "Prestige cannot exist without mystery, for people revere little what they know too well. All cults have their tabernacles, and no great man is great in the eyes of his servants." For us, that is pitching it much too strong. But there is something there, just the same, for persuaders to remember. Be free with the fun and laughter, but don't ever get silly.

To Take the Message Somewhat Obliquely. It is an odd but universal trait to enjoy sneaking a look over someone's shoulder, to be more interested or at least readier to give our attention when someone is telling something to a third party than when they are talking directly to us. Maybe this is why letters to the editor seem to attract more readers than editorials do. Similarly, as national causes have demonstrated many times, it is much easier to persuade any given state to do something because some other state has done it well than because national headquarters says it is a good idea. Alumni of the Harvard Divinity School are said to have read with more than ordinary interest a recent booklet called *What the Dean Said to the President.*

To Go for Grooves, Categories, and Easy Formulas. We may not remember things as well as we should, but we all know there were ten commandments, that Wilson had fourteen points, that our Russian friends have had lots of five-year plans, and so on. Some of the best work ever done by the American Cancer Society has been linked to the effort to teach us "cancer's seven danger signals." Whatever the reasons, it is surely clear enough that the categorical approach has at least the merit of historical endorsement.

To Reject Concepts of Debt. Uncle Sam can talk about what you owe him and get his money. But voluntary causes should know by this time that it is a sterile gambit indeed to tell prospective donors that they owe the institution something because service to them was rendered at less than cost. This has proved more than a few times to be very bad stuff indeed in college and university appeals, both with alumni and parents. There is a principle here, akin to losing your friend when you lend him money; that reproach never warms the heart or stirs the spirit.

To Suspect and Resist Change in Itself, or Any Other Implied Threat to Security. Change, it has been said by many, is always a threat to somebody's security. Anything different, more often than not, is considered suspect merely because it is different—especially, it seems, in the realm of ideas. Even in the groves of academe, as David Riesman and others have pointed out, the very persons whose life work it is to question and to differ—namely, the faculty—are usually the first to challenge innovation.

To Go with the Winning Horse. That the people love win-
ners is part of our folklore. And by now it should be one of the
accepted legends of fund-raising that support flows to promising programs rather than to needy institutions. You may
think, as too many often do, that people will rally around if
you tell them things are going badly. But they won't. You have
to whistle the happy tune and keep on the sunny side of the
street, where success lies just around the corner.

***To Pay Attention and Devote Interest in Direct Proportion
to Personal Identification.*** In the simplest possible terms, people like to see their names, have them spelled right, and have
them arranged in the way they like to have them used. Even
the agenda for a meeting gets a much more careful look, and
minutes are more apt to be read, when someone has taken the
trouble to type in the corner of every copy, "Copy for Mr. So-
and-So." (And see later remarks about subscription blanks.)

***To Revere the Past, Deprecate the Present, and Fear the
Future.*** Here, surely, is the one important tendency that needs
neither explanation nor embroidery, except to say that all this
goes right along with girth control, hefty bank balances, and
the chronic improvising of lifelong convictions.

Reviewing all these tendencies of the people, as I hope you
will from time to time, I would stress again that they all tend
especially to respond well to anything that builds *confidence*
and stirs their *pride*.

One Universal Fear

Here we have the colossal negative, so vital and so much
with us in all our problems today that it has seemed to me to
need a place to itself rather than to be included, as it might
have been, in the foregoing summary of what people tend to
do.

For there is one fear we are all born with, so deep-seated, and so universal, and so important that for our purposes here it dwarfs all others. And this one big fear is so old that the ancient Greeks had a word for it: *xenophobia,* or fear of the stranger.

Its tribal roots have plagued mankind for countless centuries, and tend to block the best of our efforts to attain the brotherhood of man by putting an end to discrimination in race, creed, and color. But it is less obvious that this instinct we all have, to beware whatever is different or strange, goes for the world of ideas as well as for the world of people.

Merely the concept of change, inevitable as it may be and pray for it as we may, always needs to be handled deftly, with the least possible reflection on the accepted leadership and the least possible damage to our nostalgic image of the good old days. And this goes for art, music, architecture, color schemes, raiment, typography, the language, and everything else with which persuaders may become involved.

SUMMARY

I hope these notes about people will have helped professionals and laity alike to understand better and remember longer:

1. Why people should be approached on at least three different levels and probably in three successive stages—beginning with the leadership, moving from the inside out, and not wasting too much time, cost, or effort at the outer periphery of the constituency.

2. What two aspirations are important to everybody.

3. Which motivations are most likely to move the moveable people to substantial action.

4. And finally, through noting what the people tend to do

and tend to fear, why any program seeking popular support should have top leadership, lofty purpose, a challenging goal with intermittent deadlines, a simple message, maximum involvement, respect and allowance for the factor of time, emphasis on continuity rather than change, an atmosphere of optimism and universality, proper rewards, and above all, every possible play for *confidence and pride.*

Professionals in particular, I would hope, will have been reminded that theirs today is a great and growing task and all the more exacting because so many people are ill informed, moved more by prejudice than by thought, and always restlessly uneasy about real or imagined threats to their secret altars. Most people, the pros should remember, don't really want to read what we write or listen to what is said, and above all don't want to have their dreams or their peace disturbed by implications of any kind that the days of their youth and the ways of their fathers were anything less than golden.

But all in all, I would beg you to believe—as I do now and always have—that most of the people are very wonderful indeed, that they almost always wish to do the right thing, and that their ultimate performance, when boldly challenged and confidently led, is usually far better than we have any right to expect. Study them and treat them well, for you need them more than money.

Chapter 2

The Makings
of a Cause

More people, more longevity, more automation; more leisure time, and more active concern for the underprivileged everywhere mean more and more of the voluntary agencies that lead and sustain current civilization. Their programs will extend further in point of time, as education is now doing with preschool and postdoctoral groups, and will surely broaden and deepen both in scope and function.

It seems equally apparent, in our ever-imperfect world, that some of these instrumentalities will be strong, and some will be weak, and that, as budget committees always find to their helpless chagrin, some are far more viable than venerable. The very good, we can assume, will have few problems. The mediocre will be with us always. But unlike the way it is with profitless business, even the very weak will seldom wither and die.

But whatever their number, their variety, their quality, or their strength, all have one big thing in common: they all have to raise money, and thus sooner or later must become a cause. And causes, I hope to show in this chapter, have unique characteristics, a few common harassments, and some accepted standards by which they may be judged, and must have at least three key qualifications in order to raise substantial sums of money.

Advocates, supporters, and prospective friends and contributors too should know about things of that sort, for their own satisfaction, to illuminate whatever it is that they choose to do, and to raise more money from more people.

The first of the unique characteristics of voluntary agencies is that they are devices peculiar to democracies. They are the swift and sure victims of tyranny and always, indeed, a reliable barometer of the democratic climate anywhere. When the Communists took over Czechoslovakia, for instance, the first move they made against voluntary services was to abolish the Boy Scouts. Certain it is that as voluntary agencies yield or gain ground, so goes freedom.

Seemingly regardless of the timing or the volume of the governmental role, another characteristic of the American voluntary agency is to lead the way. It explores new problems, sets new and higher standards, improves the quality of services, and does all the persistent probing at frontiers which traditionally has reflected American aspirations at their dynamic best. And then, after the governmental role, if any, has been set up and made to move, it is always a further characteristic of the voluntary service—primarily because it can be free, mobile, and flexible both in policy and program—to be needed every time for supplementation and emergency. The top men in Washington know this well and have nothing but good to say about the Catholic Relief Services of the National

Catholic Welfare Conference, the Church World Service, the comparable agencies of the Jews, the Friends, the Lutherans, and the Seventh-day Adventists, and the global programs of the YMCA and YWCA. All of us too should have learned our lesson on this point during the Great Depression and again during and after World War II. But alas, each succeeding generation seems to have to find this out for itself.

It is also of the very nature of all these agencies, strange as it often seems to businessmen, that their services are almost always rendered at less than cost. Function, with them, must always outrank finance. Financial support has to be there, and indeed on an ever-increasing scale, but never at the cost of independence or integrity of purpose or program. No one has put this more clearly than Harold Dodds, retired president of Princeton, when he said that it makes good sense to be solvent, but that "a college or university must live dangerously or die on the vine." No good institution would live any other way, and no good giver would have it otherwise.

Finally, in seeming contradiction to the long-established ethics of our one-price system, by which rich and poor pay the same price for the same product, all these voluntary institutions now have to seek their support—as Uncle Sam in his income tax has now done for more than fifty years—on the basis of relative income and proportionate payment. Years ago the American Red Cross financed itself by a membership program, first at $1 in dues and then at $2. But this had to be given up when costs caught up with income. St. Paul himself talked about this in his early letters, when he taught the principle that giving should be in relationship to depth of concern for the cause and relative capacity to contribute.

And then, it would ease things all around if it were more widely understood that voluntary services are commonly harassed by at least three chronic and special problems.

The first is that they are uniquely hard to manage. Perhaps this can be attributed to inborn resistance to sheer authority, to the historic objection of program people to any growth or increased power in the administrative part of the job, or to the fact that administrative leadership is more often the result of cannibalism among scholars than long-planned special training. But whatever the reasons, Cresap, McCormick, and Paget, management consultants, have summarized the difficulty in these words:

> Whereas matters of administration are the primary concern of a business excutive, they often are of secondary interest to the head of a non-profit organization.
> We have found that non-profit organizations usually are more difficult to finance, organize, and operate than business or industrial organizations of comparable size.

Next, certainly at the administrative level, virtually all of these institutions are chronically understaffed. Good staff people in the voluntary field are hard to find and always in short supply. Salary scales today are indeed more of a challenge and a reward for really top people, instead of meager bait for mediocrity. But understaffing is still such that things fail to get done that should be done or else for lack of sheer man-hours fall short of qualitative performance. Key papers on overcrowded desks can just fall off on the floor.

And then, dependent as they must be on the part-time service of volunteers, all with limited attention periods and other things to do, voluntary agencies of all kinds find it harder than you might suppose to cope with things like orderly organization, respect for channels, and adherence to time schedules. And this chronic state of affairs is often aggravated by inadequate clerical help, outmoded office equipment, cramped budgets, and even, sad to say, some of the extemporized ideas of changing lay leadership.

When it comes to evaluation by common standards, it has always seemed easier, or more inviting, to judge an agency than to run one. Every chest or united fund and probably every Better Business Bureau can offer criteria on the purpose and worthiness of agencies doing voluntary work and therefore seeking gifts. But because the matter has a place here, following are some of the stock questions:

> With what basic problem is this agency involved, and is this a problem with which I should concern myself?
>
> Just what is the agency planning to do in light of other attacks on the same problem?
>
> Is there a plan for the suggested program, and does it seem timely and well conceived?
>
> Are the trustees competent and active, and how good is the full-time leadership, and the staff assigned to the program?
>
> Does the budget seem reasonable, and have all other sources of financial aid for the program been explored and taken into account?
>
> What are others giving, especially those closest to the agency and those owing it primary loyalty and support?
>
> How much am I supposed to give, and how and when?
>
> Is such a gift proportionate to my interest in the cause, my responsibility to the agency, and my income and gifts to other causes?

Those are not all the questions, but should be enough to feed the good thought that should march hand in hand with the warm impulse.

In turn, many of the better agencies would do well to vary their classic postures of supplication just enough to declare and promote a few standards for judging the donors, such as these:

> Will this gift help advance our program or merely create new problems for us?

In limited grants from corporations and foundations, has the factor of continuity been taken into account, in some such ways as annual review, or review well in advance of termination?

Does the gift involve institutional policy, and if so, does the donor know how our policy limits gift specifications?

In grants for special programs, has an adequate allowance been made for our overhead expenses?

These questions too are more suggestive than definitive, and are meant more to provoke thought than to provide real guidance. My point is that every good gift, like every good coin, should look good on both sides.

Finally, my thesis is that every cause should be ready to show that it has relevance, importance, and urgency.

For maximum attention and response, a cause should be relevant to some major public need or problem of today and relevant also to the personal interests, loyalties, or concerns of its own natural constituency. This is obvious enough in the case of your own church, your own school or college, or your own local united fund or hospital, but sometimes it gets a little vague when a stranger with a card in his hand comes knocking at your door.

Relevance established, a cause today should have a clear image of importance. It should have importance both in its own field and within its own sphere of influence. Otherwise, with all the myriad pleas clamoring daily for attention, the agency will probably find it too difficult and relatively far too costly to do what every cause must ultimately do—catch the eye, warm the heart, and stir the mind.

My third point here is that any public cause today must establish and maintain the image of genuine urgency. It can be both relevant and important and still lose the battle if the note of obvious urgency is either obscure or merely intermittent. The mood must be one which tolerates no talk of needless compromise or costly delay and which never forgets for a moment that whatever there is plenty of time to do will probably never get done.

SUMMARY

These notes about causes should have established a few conclusions significant to all fund-raisers:

1. Voluntary services and agencies, always the lifeblood of American civilization and now fast becoming more and more important globally, call to all the best of us and the best we have for improved understanding, personal service, effective advocacy, and generous support.

2. Their policies, purposes, and programs should be paramount, with finance and fund-raising never more than means toward ends. Their campaign goals, indeed, are rarely a mere reflection of institutional ambition, but mostly a modest measurement of what they seek to do in response to modern society's own obvious and pressing needs. President Goheen of Princeton put this in the right context for everybody when he told his fellow alumni, "Much is expected of us because much is expected of Princeton."

3. Whatever we do for these agencies by word, deed, and gift and however pleasing our service to them may be in the sight of God, our performance always deserves some measurement as an act of enlightened self-interest. We need them far more than they need us. And that is what the chests have in mind when they repeat their great slogan, "Everybody benefits when nearly everybody gives."

Chapter **3**

*A*ll glory to tithers and to those who give as much or almost as much as the income tax regulations permit them to deduct. Theirs is a godly and goodly company—but a small one. For counting all individuals, the percentage of giving, as against taxable income, is still well below 4 per cent. Corporations too, allowed by law to deduct gifts up to 5 per cent of taxable income, are still giving an average of less than 1½ per cent. In short, giving is still much nearer the floor than the ceiling. And this is said, not as a reflection on our national generosity, but to make the cheerful point that there is plenty of room for growth. [4]

But if growth is to come soon enough and at the rate required, it would seem sensible for all persons interested in fund-raising to know and to remember as much as they can about current patterns for gifts and givers. They certainly should know the difference between a collection and an organized campaign. They ought to know something about the essential characteristics of the giving process and something too about different types of givers. And finally, they should at least realize how important it is to set quotas for the required numbers of dollars and gifts, if enough money is to be raised to reach campaign goals.

Loose talk plagues fund-raising in all its forms, with meandering references to "drives," "campaigns," "fund-raising programs," "marches," "crusades," "appeals," and so on. All we need to distinguish here, however, is the vital difference between a collection and an organized campaign.

A collection may have a total public goal, but has no quotas. It usually speaks for a cause, and sometimes eloquently, but says little or nothing about any specific program. It appeals to all, but to all at the same level—"Any amount will be welcome." It may have some volunteer workers, but more as carriers of cards than as informed advocates. It may ring your doorbell, but more than likely he who rings will be the postman. It may and probably does concentrate its fund-raising at some particular season or time of year; examples are the street sales around Decoration Day and the sale of stamps at Christmas and Easter. But it deals in no deadlines, and if it has any time goals, they are set by the calendar only. Its public images, mostly, are such things as benefits, coin boxes, unsolicited merchandise, wholesale mail appeals, and the like. And some fine causes have no alternatives, mainly for the reason that they have no constituencies of their own.

An organized campaign, to the contrary, seeks to finance a stated program, backs its goals by quota systems, deals with time by schedules and deadlines, and seeks to make all its volunteer solicitors well-informed and dedicated advocates. It classifies its prospect lists and directs all its procedures toward obtaining the right number of thoughtful and proportionate gifts in varying amounts at varying levels. It provides an open door for all who wish to give, but in spending time and money on field organization and on campaign materials, it is ever mindful of the law of diminishing returns. It seeks and welcomes publicity but is always aware that publicity alone seldom raises any money. Information, it concedes, is a fine thing, indeed, but never leads to action the way involvement does. Program comes first, and fund-raising is kept in its place—as a means toward an end.

The one big difference between a collection and an organized campaign, and the most significant difference in terms of raising substantial amounts of money, is thoughtful and proportionate giving, the kind that weighs the *relative importance and urgency* of the cause, the giver's own relative interest and feeling of responsibility, and his ability to give. St. Paul was doubtless the first to say anything about this, in his second letter to the Corinthians. So far as I know, community chests were the first in modern times to talk about proportionate giving, and especially when their goals as war chests skyrocketed during World War II. Annual giving funds at colleges and universities started using it after a meeting of Ivy League fund secretaries at the University Club of New York on Monday, November 21, 1949, when all eight funds decided to promote the idea by signing a joint statement about it and producing it later in their alumni magazines. "In giving to our alumni funds," they agreed to say, "let us now add careful thought to our loyalty, and discrimination to our impulse. Let us give thoughtfully and proportionately—in proportion to our concern for educational freedoms in a free society, and in proportion to our individual ability. Nothing less than that . . . can preserve this heritage that is now ours, and that we hold in trust for generations to come." Incidentally, in my opinion, this still has the makings of a good case for annual giving to education.

The giving process itself has some characteristics worth noting:

Giving Begets Giving. Chests, in World War II, had to increase their goals by a third in order to accommodate the local quotas of the National War Fund, the federation that had the job of financing the USO and all foreign relief appeals, including aid for prisoners of war. And the chests did so well at this that they raised a third more for their own local services. The same thing happened when the United Jewish Appeal was raising $100 million a year for Israel and other programs overseas. Simultaneously, it raised another third for the local goals and made possible new homes for the aged, new hospitals, schools, synagogues, and temples, and all kinds of new programs for Jewish communities in this country.

You can be just as dogmatic as you please in saying, as I will right here, that the best prospects are those who have already given and that the more a person gives, the more likely he is to give more. The best bequests usually come from the steadiest of the annual contributors. The best responses are to those workers who have made their own gifts, best of all by those workers who have talked themselves into their own responses.

The fear for purely local welfare that wants to make charity begin and end at home leads to little or no growth anywhere and certainly earns few blessings. Over and over it has been written, in all the records, that the more bread you cast on the waters the more you have for yourself.

Giving Is Primarily Responsive. People seldom give serious sums without being directly asked to do so. And this goes even for trustees and all others at the very heart of causes. They give because people at their own or a higher level ask them to give —usually more thoughtfully when asked with good reasons, more proportionately when the giving requirements are explained and the worker himself has helped set the standards, and more regularly and dependably when the contact is personal and influential. It is worthy of special note that people also tend to be responsive to the amount sought from them and seldom if ever register any kick about being given a high evaluation—for example, being told that they are thought by their peers to be among the top 10 per cent of the whole list. The cheerful fact is, on the contrary, that givers will often give more than they have intended to give when the suggestion of a respected worker aims high.

Giving Is Prompted Emotionally and Then Rationalized. The heart has to prompt the mind to go where logic points the way. The implications of this are all back there in Chapter 1, about people, especially in what was said about pride of association, concern for continuity, and confidence.

Giving Tends to Favor the Round Numbers. Individuals and corporations too, as Charles Newton of the California Institute of Technology has pointed out, tend to give by even and round numbers, like $100, $500, $1,000, and so on even into the millions. My old friend Cornelius M. Smith, one of the founders of Will, Folsom & Smith, Inc., specialists in campaigns for hospitals, originated a partial cure for such costly conformity by promoting pledge schedules calling for six payments instead of five, which, as workers could point out plausibly enough, divided much more easily into $120, $600, and $1,200. But the best way to tackle that round-number problem, as later pages here should show, is to seek help for programs instead of dollars for campaign goals.

Givers Tend to Follow Old Habit Patterns. The sound of coins dropped into collection plates, a habit most of us fell into in Sunday school, still plagues much of the giving to religion. The tambourine has helped to publicize the Salvation Army but has been a real detriment to its standards for adequate giving. Many of our best alumni, starting their annual giving to alma mater in their first years out of college, maintain their giving with more regularity than fresh thought. These are the big reasons why all fund-raisers should ask people to think about their giving and give in due proportion to their relative interest and responsibility.

Tax Talk Facilitates Giving but Is Seldom a Prime Mover. It is true enough that the more you have and the more you give, the more Uncle Sam will share the cost of your giving. But talk of taxes should never be one of fund-raising's opening moves. The place for this and for booklets about the effect of taxes on various kinds of giving is after the donor has decided to give, though perhaps before he has decided how much.

Giving Tends to Prosper Commensurately with Challenge. As Austin V. McClain, president of Marts & Lundy, Inc., (one of our oldest, biggest, and best fund-raising firms) has pointed out in a publicly available booklet and as many others have long agreed, there is little or no evidence that the ups and downs of the stock market have much appreciable effect on giving. And the big wars and catastrophes of our time have proved again that the people are always apt to give more when their lives are cued to sacrifice.

Good Giving Must Be Variable. One of the commonest maxims among all good pros is that you can't raise money adequately by the multiplication table—trying to get 1,000 persons to give $1,000 or, worse still, trying to get 10,000 persons to give $10. But you have to know your arithmetic, just the same, if you are to obtain at every level enough gifts of the right amounts to make the goal. Otherwise, the giving is all too apt to fall back into self-imposed habit patterns, the total of which has never yet reached any bold or honest objective. Especially should this factor of variability remind us that to talk of averages in organized fund-raising is to court the hemlock cup. For more people run down to an average than ever reach up to match it.

Giving Needs an Atmosphere of Optimism and Universality. Again because we all need to feel we are worthwhile members of a worthwhile group and because pride of association packs such a big punch, it naturally follows that all fund-raising—including collections—is best conducted in an atmosphere of optimism and universality. The philanthropic road sees few travelers who willingly walk alone. Most people, and I would say the rich and relatively rich in particular, usually prefer a parade.

All prospective givers eventually find their places at varying levels of the prospect-card system, in accordance with committee estimates of how much they are thought able and perhaps likely to give. But it helps to know something about the different kinds of givers, regardless of such dollar classifications.

Generally, givers tend to conform with the kinds of people discussed in Chapter 1: the leaders, the responsible, the responsive, and the inert fifth. At the top are the thoughtful minority motivated by social conscience and moved both by heart and mind. They are usually at an age of advanced maturity, are interested only secondarily in acquisition, and have an attitude about the constructive sharing of their wealth that has old roots in family or ethical tradition. They constitute not more than 5 or 10 per cent of the constituency, and in big campaigns will contribute both the leadership and all but 5 or 10 per cent of the money.

The groups following have been classified as the warm-hearted and generous, who tend to perform by the standards set for them by the leadership; the conformers, who are most apt to give when giving is clearly and inescapably part of an accepted social pattern; and at the bottom, the wholly self-centered, who give either for personal advantage or out of fear of the consequences of not giving at all. (And then there are those, when it comes to giving, who stop at nothing.)

Riches alone, it should be said, are not necessarily the mark of the good giver. There was a rich man in Philadelphia some years ago, elected to boards of high prestige in anticipation of his ultimate munificence, who used to say when solicited that he was going to start making important gifts as soon as his fortune had reached a particular level. The last level mentioned was $100 million. Then he died, and that was the end of that. There have been many like him almost everywhere, and I suppose the thing to say is that the big question is not so much the amount of money people have as how big their hearts are.

And now a closing word about the importance of quotas in gift classification. For we should know at this point that not everybody is going to give and that relatively few are going to give well. So it follows that we must ask ourselves how many gifts of what amounts are needed to reach the campaign goal.

This requires what fund-raisers usually call a "gift table," the end product of careful and experienced research and of responsible rating both at home and out in the field. And most of these tables are based on the old but still reliable rule of thumb that in any substantial capital campaign you have to get about a third of the money from the top ten gifts, another third from the next 100 largest gifts, and the last third from everybody else.

As goals have risen higher and higher, more and more has to be expected from fewer and fewer, to the point today that about 1 per cent of the list can make or break any really big campaign. However, there is astonishingly little variation in the old and simple formula of one-third, one-third, one-third.[3]

SUMMARY

Now that you have reviewed some of the background about people, their causes, and patterns taken by their current giving, a few conclusions like these should be in order:

1. Giving today has plenty of room for improvement.

2. The key to organized fund-raising is thoughtful and proportionate giving.

3. The best way to raise money is to go out and ask for it with boldness and confidence.

4. Whatever you do and however you do it, there should always be a design for giving if the giving is to match your goals.

Section 2

Campaign Procedures: Before, During, and After

What You Do Ahead of Time Is What Counts Most
Fund-Raising Techniques, Good and Bad
Postcampaign Goals and Programs

Chapter **4**

What You Do
Ahead of Time
Is What Counts Most

*P*recampaign procedures are paramount. It is what you do ahead of time and how it is done that usually decides whether you win or lose. So many shrewd laymen have observed this to be true that it is a common thing to say to a professional that if his services could be had for only one period, before or during the campaign, the preference would be for precampaign time.

This should surprise no good farmer or good tree man. For this is the time of the hoeing and the planting and the cultivation and the bending of the twig. For fund-raisers it is the time of (1) definition and design, (2) involvement in program, (3) determination of the case for the appeal, (4) selection of the leadership, and (5) setting standards for giving. These essentials should be taken care of in that order. And if they are done well, everybody can rejoice, give thanks, and sing.

Definition and Design

The first thing to do in any organized fund-raising is to make a plan. And this will involve important definitions, careful investigation, due analysis of the findings, and a number of key decisions on the campaign design.

One good man could do all this by himself but would be very foolish to try. If the project is big enough, then the best available professional help is none too good. But regardless of size, the institution should arrange at the outset for the appointment of a representative survey committee or its equivalent, if only to get the continuous benefit of the obvious advantages of participation. And the more ground such a committee covers, with more subcommittees and therefore more people involved, the more likely it is that the final report will be made as thousands cheer.

Definition, then, needs to be found for such questions as these: Just what is the problem? What do you intend to do about it? What is the audience, and is it a ready-made constituency, or do you have to create your following? What policies are involved? What is the scope of the operation, in terms of how much there is to do and how far the project must reach? What are the time factors on start, duration, and closing date? Where do you turn for authority and approvals and for help and advice? About how much is the venture apt to cost, and where is the expense money coming from? (Also to be defined at this time if not earlier are the questions of how prospects and prospective workers are to be listed and carded and how gifts are to be processed and acknowledged.)[5]

Investigation is next in order, to find the fruits of precedent and comparable experience, to seek pertinent facts and opinion that should have a bearing on what is done, and—biggest of all investigative jobs—to study the giving and working potential of the constituency. Except for purely local projects, this will involve field work. And that is the kind of work that ought to be done by the kind of people who are immune to old institutional phobias and who are in no big hurry to get home again. What I have always called "sea-gull visitation" —swooping in and out again—is no good for such field activity.

The goals sought in any precampaign investigation are (1) the identification of the power structure, the very top men and women who make anything go, (2) locating really desirable leadership, as against the easily available people who can sing and cheer but have neither the right status nor the right relationships, (3) spotting dependable workers and committee members for recommended choice and appointment later, and (4) finding out as much as possible about the probable levels of support and where any big money is coming from. All these findings should be put in writing, visit by visit, with such copies as may be desirable. Cross-indexed and studied by competent and confident people, such stuff is of a piece with gold mines.

Analysis of the findings, in light of the definitions established at the outset, should then lead to a consensus on what has to be done, how far the goal can be stretched to the point of genuine boldness, when and where the job should be launched, and about how much time it ought to take. You should have all the data, in short, with which to make your plan.

Design in fund-raising can of course be very big or very small, depending on the size of the goal, the geographical scope of the effort, the readiness of the constituency to respond, and so on. But six things belong in every plan:

First, the essence of the case for fund-raising, preferably in the form of a simple summary of the argument, rather than any attempt at deathless prose. This should reveal the aims of the program and the goals for the fund-raising and constitute an official base for all further utterances.

Second, the plan should indicate the basic structure of the campaign, in terms of identification, lines of authority, and forms of committee organization.

Third, it should state the requirements in terms of volunteer and paid personnel, card and list systems, office headquarters, campaign literature, necessary equipment, etc.

Fourth, it should lay out standards for giving in the form of tables showing the needed number of gifts of varying amounts and should specify the workings of some practical quota system, by which the job of solicitation can be broken up into manageable work units locally, by committees, teams, and individual workers. The quota concept generally is basic to all functions, as a challenge and measurement for performance of any kind.

Fifth, surely every plan needs a time schedule.

And sixth, every plan should have an approved expense budget, with directions for making it work.

These few specifics of design should always be insisted upon, and should find substantial agreement among all those with top authority. And then you will be ready for the next pre-campaign move—involvement in program.

Involvement in Program

Ideally, all voluntary institutions should be involving their constituencies in program at all times, and not merely when funds are to be raised. The agencies of community chests and united funds usually do this well, from many years of experiencing the fruits of it. Many churches do it well, and voluntary hospitals are now enrolling men as well as women and girls. The chapter workrooms of the American Red Cross, as previously pointed out, breed more fund-raising loyalty than all the booklets ever written, and many colleges and universities these days have as many as 10 per cent of their alumni involved in recruiting, club work, and annual fund collections.

To be stressed here is merely the point that taking a hard look at the involvement process is a key step in the precampaign period, a step that should be taken at the earliest possible time, seeking in particular personal identification with the program, as widely as may be necessary, among all those in a position to do the cause the most good by word, deed, and gift.

Involvement, most of the old pros like to say, is more important than information; for information, alas, can be ignored. Involvement is universal and starts early. It begins, as Professor Bruner of Harvard found in experiments with babies only fifteen months old, with movement toward the object—no movement, no interest. And what it means is that all people start committing themselves to personal identification at the moment they make a move that expresses open interest or desire. That, we may be sure, is why the tent evangelist always wants the converts to come forward.

The visiting committees of the Harvard Board of Overseers are a prime example of the involvement process at a high level, as are the Princeton Today programs, their counterparts at the University of Michigan and elsewhere, and indeed all the recent councils at the Vatican. And you should note about these examples that while the participants do have to do a lot of listening, they are not merely captive audiences. Dialogue gets in the act as well as monologue, and you should put that down as something very big indeed.

And don't be overawed. Involvement can be big stuff, but it can and should be simple too. For just as I have always felt that the best public relations are the aggregate of many tremendous trifles, so it is that personal identification can be sought and won by the persistent application of procedures like this:

Seek their advice or opinion.   Seek their testimony.
Promote meaningful visitation.   Use their names.
Ask them to join something.   Take their pictures.
Quote them, with adequate visi-   Send advance proofs.
   bility.   Pay attention.
Ask them to make a speech.

Simplest of all, perhaps, ask them to do something for you. At any rate, be thinking about the process as the most dependable way to develop advocacy and support at the maximum level, preferably all the time but especially in the precampaign period.

Determination of the Case

The essence of the case for fund-raising, as determined during the original process of definition and design, will have been enough for establishing agreement among those in control with regard to the program to be financed and the list of needs comprising the campaign goal. But something more will then be required for the enlistment of leadership, the enrollment of workers, and the solicitation of the first pace-setting gifts.

The basic document for this purpose has come to be known as the "case statement." And this is the one definitive piece of the whole campaign. It tells all that needs to be told, answers all the important questions, reviews the arguments for support, explains the proposed plan for raising the money, and shows how gifts may be made and who the people are who vouch for the project and will give it leadership and direction.

Sheer length here is no automatic evil. Those who read this piece will actually want to read it and will really need to know what it says, both as the basis for their own understanding and as the official source book for all subsequent speeches and campaign literature. Which is all the more reason why the tone and content of the job should reflect creditably on the taste and image of the institution and its leaders.

Above all, such statements need to be carefully planned, or briefed. Usually they are not, with the melancholy result that first drafts are often in the wrong sequence, tend to contain the unnecessary, omit the essential, and disregard far too much of what we ought to know about people. It also happens too frequently that the writer seems to get so involved with his hymns of hyperbole that he overlooks what one of my professors called "the tremendous emphasis of understatement." To these people I usually say that if the piece has simplicity, good taste, and logical order, the eloquence should be allowed to find its way in, as beauty does in the eye of the beholder.

Finally, it should be said that the case for fund-raising—taking into account what has been said about people, causes, and giving—should aim high, provide perspective, arouse a sense of history and continuity, convey a feeling of importance, relevance, and urgency, and have whatever stuff is needed to warm the heart and stir the mind.

Incidentally, this will be the time to decide on the plan's recommendations for campaign literature.

And aside from the case statement itself, often in typewriter type with a special cover in color, and the special presentations to be done for key individuals and for foundations and big corporations, my view about campaign literature is that it should be planned in light of these four essential functions:

Summarization. Every campaign, big or little, needs, in addition to the case statement, a printed piece fitting easily into purse or pocket, reciting swiftly the essence of purpose, program, and need, covering the points of importance, relevance, and urgency, and making the case both for thoughtful and proportionate giving and for payment over a period of at least three years in capital campaigns—with enough respected names aboard to evoke confidence. In some campaigns, this will be all the printed literature actually needed; all too often it is the only piece to be read and heeded. Workers always like such a piece, and sometimes it doubles in brass as a mailing enclosure in the cleanup period. In any event, this is a piece deserving the best available attention in its planning, writing, layout, printing, and plan of distribution.

Visualization. If buildings are involved, or much new personnel not well known to the constituency, ways must be found to let people see what and whom you are talking about. This may mean a map, slides, possibly a movie (though movies are often just a sure way to spend a lot of money for an uncertain result), and perhaps a special piece loaded with good pictures. But whatever methods are chosen, two warnings are in order. Don't be led into *avant-garde* art work unfamiliar to your bifocal audience. And second, don't assume that the old-timers will know as much as you think they do about the details of locale; those who remember the least will be the last to confess it and the first to resent their predicament.

Arousing the Good Sentiment. As I have said before, to stir the mind to go where logic points the way, the heart of the giver must first be warmed. Best of all, we should arouse pride of association and a feeling of responsibility for the continuity. And so how do you go about a thing as delicate as this without getting stuck in just plain goo?

The answer is to be found in the appropriate use of music, pertinent quotations, speeches or statements by the right people, dramatizations of function through colorful ceremonies based on youthful participation of one kind or another, and measures that evoke the best that has gone, pride for the present, and warm promise for the future.

Success in athletics is no answer. But Brooks Atkinson found the key in Harvard's successful campaign for $82 million by persuading thirty-nine Harvard men of differing ages and interests to write brief essays on how they felt about their college and what they believed it gave them. This was put together in a little book called *College in a Yard,* and while it said nothing anywhere about money or giving to Harvard, it turned out by common consent as the one great blockbuster in warming up the campaign workers to do their jobs as well as they did. I read it, and I lay awake many a night later, trying to think of what I might have said had Atkinson asked me to testify too. And you just can't stir things up much better than that.

Not every cause can have such a printed piece, nor is it always necessary to plan for deliberate heart warmers. But the function is nonetheless vital, and should never be overlooked in the scheduling and creation of the campaign literature and in judgments on art and copy.

Keeping the Continuity. No function of the campaign literature can be more important than sustaining both the mood of importance, relevance, and urgency and an atmosphere of optimism and universality. And the function becomes more and more important as campaign goals go higher and higher and schedules have to cover more and more time. For as solicitation moves from the inside out, from one group of givers to another, and as the limited number of traveling teams of official advocates go from section to section and city to city, the risk of having the campaign die on some vines becomes a real thing indeed.

The key to this problem is that the voice of authority must keep talking. After the original statement, the ultimate boss can never let up until the task has been completed. Never should he make a speech or write a report without referring to the unfinished task with all the gravity due its importance and with the open courage and confidence worthy of certain and complete success. What he says and keeps saying is important in itself and almost equally important in that he says it and never lets up.

Another form of continuity insurance is multiple exposure. Other administrative people, in speeches and articles for public consumption, should remember always that the constituency can hardly be expected to feel more strongly about the campaign than they apparently do and that there cannot be effective advocacy that is either casual or intermittent. Editors of alumni magazines sometimes overlook this principle in their anxiety to keep their columns independent of administrative control and daintily free of too much talk about money.

Continuity is also the main business of campaign bulletins, which sometimes make the mistake of dealing almost solely with progressive statistics. My feeling has always been that these bulletins are worthy of more careful planning than they usually get, to the end that every issue should deliberately touch certain specific bases—attainment of higher standards, involvement of respected persons, outside praise, comparable successes by comparable institutions, evidence of significant campaign growth, quotations worthy of repetition, and every good thing that can make for confidence.

Not discussed here are tax leaflets, handbooks for committee members, memorial brochures, and that most traditional printed piece of all, the "major pamphlet." I have nothing against any of these pieces, and have written lots of them myself. But just how many biscuits they ever butter would be hard to prove. So that is why I say campaign literature should be planned in light of function and likelihood of being read and heeded.

The Vital Role of Leadership

Where to list the step of selecting leadership is often puzzling. For sheer importance, it belongs in first place. But the case for fund-raising usually wins that spot merely because you need the best possible case in order to enlist the best possible leadership. And if there is any one thing you really have to have in successful fund-raising, that is it; *exciting* leadership, many would say—the kind that knows you can't hope to borrow their ears if you're merely going to lend your name.

The temptation to throw in a few hefty negatives right here is too strong to resist.

Leadership is not just ornamentation. It is not merely what Mencken used to call "inherited respectability." And it is not the oracle who would a pundit be, by evermore giving himself to the improvising of lifelong convictions. Men such as these, always to be found in all communities, have the bombast but no bombs. They like to be where the pomp is, but not the pump. In short, whatever else they may be, they can preside but they can never lead.

Now the right kind of leadership, on the other hand, is exciting in itself and exciting to write about. We have only to recall the immortal story of Winston Churchill—before, during, and after World War II—to note that great leadership seems to have an affinity for the great event and the mighty crisis. And the cheerful meaning of this for fund-raisers is that the bigger the cause may be and the bolder its objectives, the more likely it is that a top leader will somehow emerge.

Such men are of course rare. But they are always worth looking for and worth waiting for. They bring warmth and confidence to the cause. They have a way of attracting the interest and the loyalty of effective and devoted lieutenants. They give the required amount of their talents and their time, the best of them realizing, I think, that there is nothing more dangerous than the second-class attention of a first-class man. They know what the committee system is for and how to use it. And finally, by the example of their own words, deeds, and gifts, they help to set high standards of campaign performance and thus invoke a broad and adequate response of enthusiastic and sacrificial support. They never question the good faith of those with other views, and they never doubt the ultimate victory.

James F. Oates, Jr., chairman of Princeton's great campaign for $53 million which raised more than $60 million, put it well and spoke as the matchless prototype he surely is, when he said at a campaign meeting, "The shadows will always be behind those who walk toward the light."

Where do you find such paragons?

Generally, campaign leadership should be found in the family. In fact, one fair and good way to measure any institution is to see whether it has on its board of trustees or somewhere close to the heart of things a man who has what leadership takes. If not, indeed, some real institutional shuffling may be in order.

But many causes, without the obvious constituencies of long-established institutions, have to look farther afield. Their case, in seeking leadership, must depend on interest in the problem and the cause rather than on loyalty or devotion to the institution itself. And that means looking where the public interest is strongly involved and is recognized in terms of a public relations policy favoring the participation of top men in public affairs. I can think of no better example of this than the Bell System, which, on the appeal of John D. Rockefeller,

Jr., to Walter S. Gifford, came up with Chester I. Barnard, president of the New Jersey Bell Telephone Co., to be president of the USO in those vital early days of 1942. (After the war, the USO was similarly aided by Carl Whitmore, then president of the New York company.)

Not all causes, naturally enough, can hope to enlist campaign leadership of such national distinction, nor do they need to. But even in local causes and those with relatively modest goals and limited constituencies, the principle holds true that the place to look for leaders is where public interest ranks high. The new head of a local bank seeking growth, the newcomer who has been brought in to head an important business and needs broad acquaintance and prompt recognition, the young lawyer in quest of favorable visibility within the strictures of his legal ethics, the holder of the district franchise for bottling and distributing popular soft drinks—all these and their comparable counterparts are among the suitable and likely candidates. But whatever the man's ranking and whatever the cause, the main thing to look for here is the kind of natural and honorable motivation that leads to first-class attention.

And this you are most apt to find among those who are always busy and often "too busy." Retired men, in fact, are usually bad risks for hard and effective leadership, perhaps because influence tends to wane with retirement and loss of leverage but more likely because older men, as I know so well, are apt to have lost their zeal for the long hour, the hard swing, and the chicken and peas of the campaign tours.

One other warning is very much in order.

The courtship of good leadership is seldom easy, and may necessitate approaching a whole series of choices. The warning is to keep all such hunts inviolable secrets. For when the word gets around that several have been asked and have turned the job down, the difficulty of enlisting the right kind of leadership becomes needlessly compounded and sometimes insurmountable.

Jefferson had a dream of the leadership of an aristocracy of talent. For important fund-raising, such dreams are none too high. Strong faith is what you need, and a bearing of boldness and confidence. Perhaps finding and nurturing such leadership and being content with nothing less constitute fund-raising's greatest art of all.

Setting Standards for Giving

You don't have to be a golfer to realize that practically everything we try to do is by the par and bogey system. In business, politics, sports, and even in religion, we look at the old record, establish fresh targets, and shoot for the new mark. And this gets you into the very vitals of organized fund-raising—giving standards and quota systems.

Happily, these are two subjects that lend themselves freely to a double dose of dogma. For while many things about fund-raising are either debatable or obscure, here I can and shall speak ex cathedra:

First, all organized fund-raising has to have analysis of the total potential in terms of careful rating for the best of the individual prospects and then, based on that study, a system of quotas. Otherwise, you can't establish the right goal, you can't break that total goal down into local targets, and no giver can know what the gift requirements are.

Second, all quota systems for capital campaigns, allowing of course for reasonable flexibility, should be based on that rule of three explained in Chapter 3 (page 32), to the effect that about one-third of the money has to come from the top ten gifts, another third from the next 100 gifts, and the last third from all other gifts. The size of the goal is the big modifier here, but even in the very big campaigns the proportions hold true astonishingly well. In Princeton's case, the top ten gifts gave 27½ per cent, the next 100 gifts 39 per cent, and all others 33½ per cent. At Harvard the top ten gave 28 per cent, the next 100 gave 38 per cent, and all others gave 34 per cent. (See accompanying gift tables, for what was expected and what happened.)[6]

GIFT TABLES FOR THE CAPITAL CAMPAIGNS OF PRINCETON AND HARVARD

$53,000,000 for Princeton University:

Projection of gifts needed from all sources to attain goal and actual results

	Needed		Received	
Size of gift	Approximate no. donors	Approximate amount	No. donors	Amount
$1,000,000 and over	10	$15,000,000	9	$16,165,396
100,000 and over	100	18,000,000	107	24,543,879
10,000 and over	500	10,000,000	499	10,723,475
1,000 and over	3,000	7,000,000	3,208	6,887,380
Under 1,000	17,000	3,000,000	14,102	2,391,237
Total	20,610	$53,000,000	17,925	$60,711,367

Program for Harvard College:

$10,000,000 and up	1	$10,000,000	None	None
5,000,000-9,999,999	2	12,000,000	None	None
1,000,000-4,999,999	7	10,000,000	15	$30,127,169
100,000- 999,999	110	29,000,000	115	27,144,352
50,000- 99,999	100	5,000,000	45	2,867,100
10,000- 49,999	500	9,000,000	537	9,704,376
5,000- 9,999	400	3,000,000	519	3,119,944
1,000- 4,999	1,500	2,000,000	3,408	5,743,472
Less than 1,000	20,000	2,500,000	23,124	3,814,105
Group-gift donors			3,933	255,036
Total	22,620	$82,500,000	31,696	$82,775,554

Third, quota performance works best from the inside out, beginning with the active and retired members of the governing board, proceeding next to the 100 gifts of the highest amount, then through the 500 best prospects, and after that proceeding regionally and locally on the solicitation of the last third of the money. Final quotas for local purposes should not be set until there has been enough demonstration of giving patterns to lend the final figures some basis for confidence and ready acceptance. And how far any institution wishes to extend its fund-raising periphery in the final solicitation of smaller gifts should depend on the factors that go beyond the raising of money in itself, such as constituency relationships, cultivation of local clubs, preparation for better annual giving programs, laying foundations for a bequest program, and so on.

Fourth, quotas should be established at every level, down to every single team in every local campaign. United funds and community chests and most hospital campaigns are far ahead in the employment of this technique. But what they do, and our Jewish friends too, anyone can do: they simply base their team quotas on the "card values"—the total conservatively to be expected from the assigned prospects after rating each individual card.

Fifth, all quota systems need cushions. For while some giving will be above expected levels (there is an old tradition that every big campaign will have at least one big windfall gift), some giving will fall below. Prudence indicates that all the separate quotas should quietly add up to something more than the public goal, preferably to as much as 120 per cent, or as much as the traffic will bear. Moreover, the cushion principle should apply to the number of prospects required for the needed number of gifts at each level. At the top, for instance, there should be four or five prospect cards for every needed gift.

Sixth, within the limits of practical operation, people

should be told, not how much they should give, but how much you hope they will want to give or what others at their level are giving. This is consistent with what was said back there on page 30, with what St. Paul told the Corinthians, and with the famous advice of Benjamin Franklin: "Apply to all those whom you know will give something; next to those whom you are uncertain whether they will give anything or not; and show them the list of those who have given: and lastly, do not neglect those you are sure will give nothing; for in some of them you may be mistaken."

So much for the dogma about setting the standards of giving. I would suggest, with the assurance of a unanimous professional chorus, that you regard it as gospel and read it at least twice. But there are also some things to add here about procedures, especially those having to do with goals and quota systems. For in all this, giving standards are deeply involved.

Goal setting in chest campaigns often follows a rule of seeking about 3 per cent more than was raised the year before and then fighting hard to raise no less than 97 per cent of the new campaign objective. Borrowing Herman Hickman's wonderful line about Yale football and Yale's alumni, this tends to keep the agencies "sullen but not mutinous."

Whatever the cause or circumstances, campaigns for annual giving have to raise about 3 per cent more every year just to keep trotting alongside inflation and growth of the constituency.[7] But with rare exceptions, nothing short of national crisis or obvious calamity can make these annual appeals take great and sudden leaps upward. The chests, the church causes, the health agencies, and the best of the alumni funds can only expose and expound their long-term aspirations, appeal consistently to pride of association and concern for continuity, and keep plugging away for thoughtful, proportionate, and dependable support.

The very habit patterns here that can be so frustrating can also be a continuing comfort; for while about half the givers tend to come up with the same amount they gave the previous year and around 15 per cent tend to give less, there is usually a dependable 10 per cent of new givers or givers who had lapsed and have come home again and a warmly welcomed 25 per cent who give more than they gave the year before. Whatever else anyone wants to say about this somewhat viscous performance, it does make for the steady climb, and it also lays secure foundations for increased bequests and occasional special gifts. And the total figures continue to mount.

My own conclusion is that the top campaign goal in any annual campaign is not nearly as important as the dozens or hundreds of goals that get established down through organization channels in terms of unit quotas. It's the successful battles that win the war.

Goal setting in capital campaigns is quite different. And here I shall lean heavily, if not actually go piggyback, on the special talents and long experience of my old friend and colleague Carl A. Kersting. Now the head man at Kersting, Brown & Co., one of the top fund-raising firms, he learned about quotas and devised much of the technique of establishing quota systems in the days of World War II, in the first two USO campaigns and then in the three years of the National War Fund. Lately, he has been responsible for some almost uncanny predictions in several of the biggest capital campaigns that have ever been run.

So with Carl's special guidance, here is a fast summary of what to do in setting goals for capital campaigns:

The first step is to put the suggested goal to the test of

the rule of thirds. Is it likely that the cause can obtain ten gifts accounting for at least one-third of the money? Again, is it likely that the next 100 donors will give at least another third? And that the top 500 gifts will yield more than 90 per cent of the suggested goal?

Another initial test is a realistic guess at how much the governing board will give. This is coming to be known as the trustees nucleus fund, and while a yield of at least 15 per cent of the goal is considered important—and in smaller campaigns much more than that—the really vital consideration is unanimity of response at an obviously sacrificial level. The leverage of influence on the campaign is the quality of the response, and not primarily the number of dollars. In fact, no initial response from the governing board should be considered final, for in virtually all recent cases the final amount given by present and former trustees has been at a substantially higher figure—sometimes twice the original total or more.

Obviously, these procedures call for rather accurate evaluation of the prospective contributors. And at the Golden Jubilee Conference of the American Alumni Council, at Atlantic City on July 11, 1963, here is what Kersting had to say about that, addressing his remarks particularly, of course, to colleges and universities:

> Get the records of donors who in the last ten years, at any one time, have given the institution $500 or more. Then have the class agents evaluate these cards for capital purposes, and suggest other names that should be added.
>
> Check the resulting list in the field by personal interviews with trustees and leading alumni, both for ability to give and degree of probable interest—at the same time seeking new names.
>
> Seek further data on now much each top prospect is prob-

ably worth through S.E.C. reports, proxy statements, and so on; the point being that it is both unfair and ineffective to expect a solicitor to aim high without all possible information about the target. When assignments are made, complete information—confidential, of course—should be available concerning all the top prospects.

Finally, Kersting makes the important point that the membership of top committees should be held open until the prospect evaluation has been completed. For the best kind of solicitors often turn up in that process—those whose own contributions tend to elevate and sustain high standards of giving.

Only two more things about giving standards occur to me as important to mention here.

One is that the amount of the dollars alone is never as significant as the right gift coupled with the right giver. Good examples are of the knowledgeable and discriminating giver, as John D. Rockefeller, Jr., was known to be for so many years, and the obviously sacrificial gift, like the unexpectedly large pledge of a relatively impecunious college president.

My other point is that good examples should be sought not merely at the top but at every level, preferably to the end that every single quota will have a guiding gift to light its way.

SUMMARY

Plato said, "The beginning is the most important part of the work." Whatever else you may have gotten out of this chapter, I hope you can now see why what you do ahead of time is what counts most. After that, I would hope you now find yourself in agreement with these five conclusions:

1. The first step is to define the problem, search out the pertinent facts and opinions, and make a plan for the campaign design, with plenty of representative help and concurrence.

2. Constantly, and certainly as early as possible in the precampaign stage, institutions should work hard for effective involvement in program, especially among those in a position to do the cause the most good.

3. Good planning should make sure that the case for fund-raising does what a good case is supposed to do: cover the ground, aim high, catch the eye and ear, warm the heart, and then stir the mind to the convinced conclusion that the cause has importance, relevance, and urgency.

4. Never settle the leadership for anything less than the first-class attention of a first-class man, preferably somebody with incandescent eyeballs, but above all somebody who evokes faith and confidence because he always has more than enough of both to spare.

5. And finally, it will be found that the measurements of victory depend on the giving standards and the quota systems; from the inside out and at each successive level of the campaign.

So now, with all that behind you, you should be ready to consider some of fund-raising's standard techniques, good and bad.

Chapter 5

Fund-Raising Techniques, Good and Bad

$\mathscr{A}$t this stage there should be an accepted plan, a time schedule, and a budget. The leadership should be all fired up and ready to go. It should be known who the right workers are, how many are needed, and how to get them. The giving constituency should have been identified and rated for interest and giving ability. There should also be enough pace-setting gifts, of the right amounts to set standards for giving and to establish quotas. Hopefully, both involvement and cultivation will be well advanced.

Much will therefore have been done, and much will lie ahead. It may be helpful to you to consult from time to time the accompanying check list for the common difficulties and even to go back and take another look at these chronic troubles after you have finished this chapter. But of course the thing to do here is to accent the positive.

CHECK LIST FOR THE COMMON DIFFICULTIES

Case may be faulty, with one or more of these weaknesses:
  Too institutional and thus with too little *relevance.*
  Too much accent on need rather than opportunity.
  Too little rationale, in terms of importance and urgency.
  Too little basis for confidence by indication of long and expert planning, competence of team to operate the plan, and probable viability.
  Too much dependence on one-shot explanation, with too little allowance for repetition.
  Too much catering to colleagues rather than audience.

Leadership may be weak on both lay and professional levels:
  Too many *names* and too few workers.
  Too little attention to *competence of lieutenants.*
  Too little dependence on committee functions, importance of meetings, validity of deadlines, etc.
  Too much easy settling for second-rate help.

Procedures may be ineffective, in these basic ways:
  Too much dependence on information and not enough on *involvement.*
  Too much accent on minor motivations and side issues.
  Too little insistence on planned sequences and hence too much shooting from the hip.
  Not enough distinction between activity and accomplishment.
  Too little optimism, dramatization, universality, recognition, and persistence.

So here we go on fund-raising's good techniques, approximately in the order in which they have to be considered:

Headquarters

The old rule, and a good one, is that the campaign headquarters should be where the chairman is, which more often than not is where there is also a strong concentration of the constituency.

Temporary as the arrangements must be, the amount of space is dictated largely by what is available—free if possible, but in any event at the lowest possible cost. A rule of thumb is that you need 200 square feet for the first person and at least 100 square feet for each additional person.

In recent years, with higher goals, there has been a marked tendency in university campaigns toward decentralization, in terms of more field offices. Harvard's original campaign, in 1919, had offices only in Boston and New York, whereas the Program for Harvard College, with a goal six times greater, had offices in Boston, New York, Washington, Chicago, and Cleveland, and on the West Coast. Princeton had seven offices, and Cornell's centennial campaign had ten. And these are records not likely to last very long when the big universities in the Middle West get their capital campaigns under way.

Policy here depends on purpose. For fund-raising only, not many offices are needed. But if a cause or an institution has other goals in mind, such as cultivation of the entire constituency, the only practical limit to the number of field offices is the perennial difficulty of finding competent people to staff them.

The most effective economy for any campaign headquarters is to set a high enough salary scale to get first-class secretarial and clerical help. One top person is worth at least three bumblers and costs a lot less—in more ways than one. Furniture can be borrowed (but the equipment should be first class), rented, leased, or purchased with a buy-it-back arrangement. The campaign treasurer or the depository bank should supervise the system for accounting and handling of gifts, provided the need for speed is duly recognized. Any good office manager will know what the office routines should be.

But my final word of advice here is that there should always be a written set of rules covering the public relations of headquarters operation—prompt answers for mail, immediate exposure of error, no buck passing, courtesy for all callers, and nobody ever in conference.

Prospect Listing

I must state here, of course, that prospect listing is of the utmost importance. Beyond that, I feel much as the Wright brothers would have felt if someone at Kitty Hawk had asked them how to reach the moon.

The techniques and equipment have changed so much, and are still changing with bewildering rapidity. Only an office-systems expert of today or some reputable fund-raising firm with broad experience can now give you the last word.

So I will go no farther than to say that every campaign needs a master file with the cards in alphabetic order, sometimes called a "locator file," and enough subordinate card files to serve both the purposes of class or local identification and the prospect groupings after the rating has been done— select, special, general, and so on. (See accompanying sample card.)[5]

So-called "flat" lists, typed on sheets, are usually needed too, especially for prospect selection by the volunteer solicitors and for keeping track of assignments.

NAME	AREA	ASSIGNED TO	CODE

BUSINESS ADDRESS	DIRECTORSHIPS

TYPE OF BUSINESS	
TELEPHONE SEC'Y	
RESIDENCE	

TELEPHONE	MEMBERSHIPS
OTHER ADDRESS	

MAILINGS	PRINCETON RELATIVES

PROSPECT'S SALUTATION DATE OF BIRTH	RELIGION	POLITICS

FATHER'S NAME	MOTHER'S MAIDEN NAME		
WIFE'S MAIDEN NAME	MARRIED	SALUTATION	EDUCATION
CHILDREN	BIRTHDATE	MARRIED TO	EDUCATION

PRINCETON UNDERGRADUATE ACTIVITIES

OTHER EDUCATIONAL HISTORY

PRINCETON COMMITTEE AFFILIATIONS & DATES	PRINCETON TODAY

PRINCETON CONTACTS	INTERESTS & HOBBIES	ESTIMATED WEALTH

Sample card (front).

NAME		AREA		ASSIGNED TO	CODE
		GIFTS OVER $100 SINCE 7/1/59		ADDITIONAL DATA & CULTIVATION	
DATE	AMOUNT		DATE	REMARKS	ANNUAL GIVING
		CUMULATIVE TOTAL PRIOR 7/1/59			59/60
		$53M			60/61
					61/62
					62/63
					63/64
					64/65
					65/66
					66/67
					67/68
					68/69
					69/70
					70/71
					71/72
					72/73
					73/74
					74/75
					75/76
					76/77

GENERAL

Sample card (back).

"Stop cards" is the trade term for the important device of pulling out prior to any assignment meeting all the top names reserved for special handling and replacing these cards with cards of another color, marked "reserved" or "assigned." Called stop cards, these substituted cards are supposed to keep the names of the best prospects away from less influential workers.

Like a priest with his breviary, every campaign director should spend some time every day in loving and devoted review of the top layer of his prospect list. Always should he know who the next ten top prospects are and what is being done about them.

This brief section, I should say, is written on the supposition that the cause has its own identified constituency, with reasonably accurate names and addresses. If not, Herculean list labors lie in wait—and incidentally a very tough campaign. In such cases you need the very best help you can get, if you can persuade them to work for you, and much more than the usual amount of time and expense.

One final reminder—arrange names the way the people want theirs arranged, and make sure the spelling is without a flaw. (John Price Jones, my boss for many years, was never J. P. Jones or John P. Jones, but John Price Jones—the whole works.)

Basic Materials

Aside from the campaign literature dealt with in the previous chapter (page 44), the first item that comes to mind here is the subscription blank, or pledge card.

Those who make the larger gifts usually write letters, of transmittal or declaration of intent. They seldom use an ordinary subscription blank. But for general purposes every fund-raising campaign needs a standard form—as a prop or conversation piece for the worker, as a dotted line for consummating the gift transaction, and also, I have always thought, as the final piece in the chain of sale. This means that the subscription-card copy deserves the best available thought, and not merely the dull and antiseptic phrases of legal terminology. It should restate the big purpose, perhaps by summarizing the needs on the back, should evoke confidence by the use of at least a few influential names, should suggest universality by some such device as "I *too* wish to safeguard . . . ," and should imply that serious giving is in order by always planting the thought that gifts of securities are not uncommon—"Checks *and securities* should be made payable to. . . ." And if time and facilities make it possible, the prospect's name and address should be typed on the card or blank in advance, so that it will not be just any old card, but his card.

Visual Aids

With me, visual aids start with check lists—such as those included in this book. They are useful reminders and help mightily to keep things in the right order. And then up on the wall you can have an organization chart, with names to be filled in as enlistment and organization proceed, a meetings and events calendar, a schedule for campaign mailings, and perhaps one of those big maps on which pins of various colors can indicate all the ways in which great good is being done.

Most useful of all, in annual giving, is a campaign progress chart, showing week by week the total dollars reported and possibly the total number of gifts. The American Cancer Society has kept such a dollar chart from April 1 to September 1 ever since 1945, and my old friend there, economist Harold Barkan, tells me that at the end of eight or nine weeks its curves still predict with astonishing accuracy what the final total will be at the end of August. (Incidentally, the chart also carries the happy message that the total raised in the society's annual Crusade grew from $4,292,491 in 1945 to $36,920,999 in 1965.)[8]

We kept such a chart for the three years of the National War Fund (1943–1945), and we found even in that short time that for the reporting period of sixteen weeks, the total around the fourth and fifth week proved to be substantially half of the amount finally reported and that the total at the end of the eighth week, or halfway mark, always turned out to be more than 90 per cent of the final total. Which ought to be still more proof that it's what you do ahead of time that counts most.

Top Organization

The originating group in any campaign, it has been said for many years, should represent all the important elements of the giving constituency: the political groupings, the three major faiths, the differing age groups, women as well as men, varying social levels, and, in national campaigns, state and regional representation.

But these are scenic effects only, and all alone lead nowhere. Some may remember American Overseas Aid, launched soon after World War II and dedicated to a most worthy and timely cause. It had all the top organization anyone could want and a number of state and local chairmen too. But it was top-heavy in its organization, with no established constituency at the grass roots—like the church organizations, with their dioceses and local parishes, or the colleges and universities, with their alumni, or the National War Fund, indeed, with its tie-ups with local chests and war funds. American Overseas Aid strove mightily but raised less than a million.

The most important element in organization, with the scenery all set, is influence, and the other big element is action. Sponsorship, for instance, is fine for creating confidence, and confidence you must have. But the dynamics never come without influence and action.

The best way to get influence, in any kind of a campaign, is to seek out the power structure. And everywhere, in all communities, the power structure comprises these four groups: those who have inherited both wealth and a tradition of public service; the newly rich and newly powerful, the Horatio Algers of the modern world; the top professional managers of key corporations; and what John Kenneth Galbraith calls "men of standing," in his charming reminiscences of boyhood years in Ontario (*The Scotch,* Houghton-Mifflin).

These men are always there. They conform to similar standards, follow and respect the patterns of habitual success, patronize the same resorts, and—what is important to us here—are very likely to know each other, clear across the board. These are the men among whom leaders are to be found, at all levels, and among whom executive committees are to be recruited. They have the influence. And then good management can produce the action.

No one, I think, has written more interestingly about the power structure than Patrick J. Nicholson, vice-president of the University of Houston and now president of the American College Public Relations Association. He wrote a piece for the association's *Journal,* the winter issue of 1962, called "The Special Giver in the Power Structure of the Community." It was so full of good stuff that one hardly knows where to pick and quote. But here is a paragraph helpful both for organization work and for rating of workers and prospects:

> One of the easiest means of identifying most elements of the power structure, and of working over a prime prospect list, is to spend an afternoon incommunicado in the office of an alumnus or other avid supporter who really knows the community and area. One of the very best candidates for such an endeavor is a former chairman of the United Fund, or a member of the rating committee for these campaigns. I have watched such a man—admittedly one with a remarkable memory—run through 500 cards in a half day while he ticked off such statistics as probability of a contribution, asking range, current state of the prospect's business, specific contact within an organization, and best worker for the card. These are the golden hours which restore health, vigor, and confidence in free enterprise.

Dr. Nicholson also points out in this piece a new and useful idea: having persons on the staff who specialize in the genealogy of the area power structure.

> Inasmuch as there is a considerable amount of intermarriage at the upper socioeconomic level, or what a cynical friend of mine calls the dynastic merger, it can be vital to know these interrelationships.

The power structure, certainly, leads to quality and influence, and in neither of these respects are sheer numbers of much importance. Lenin's advice, "Reduce the membership and strengthen the Party," is directly applicable to the executive side of organized fund-raising. And so is the dictum that the ways of effective voluntary organization are seldom the ways of democracy. You don't elect people for this work; you pick them.

And when the inevitable blocks or bottlenecks show up, as they are certain to do, you let them stand right there unmolested while you go about setting up the bypass. The executive committee has died on the vine? You create a steering committee and operate from there, humbly thanking Ultimate Authority for the flexibility and resourcefulness of our wonderful English language.

Under the management level, organization usually follows the natural patterns of operating function as laid out in the campaign plan. But if the appointment of a public relations or publicity committee happens to be overlooked, no cosmic harm will be done. They are fine stuff indeed for opening doors in all sorts of media, but should seldom if ever mess around with copy. My own old rule is that the fewer who pass on copy, the better the chances will be of saving the golden words from the mediocrity of multiple compromise.

Organization always needs good supervision and periodic reindoctrination. It also needs a simple framework of purpose and policy, with defined objectives and functions. And as we shall soon see, it also needs meetings and reports.

Workers

The American Association of Fund-Raising Counsel says that in all these United States there are about fifty million volunteer workers. And I think the first thing to do with a whopping generalization like that, impressive and roughly accurate as it may be, is to slice it up into a few comprehensible and meaningful realities.

For one thing, as far as committee work is concerned,

most people clearly prefer the pursuit of happiness to the happiness of pursuit. Only about a third of those who enroll, in the experience of many and in the words of my old friend and colleague, Wolcott D. Street, perform with little prodding; another third act "effectively or moderately so, with some needling"; and the other third "are no good at all and not worth the time to call them up." (An actual experience in a very large, very prestigious, and very successful capital campaign, as well managed as expert direction could make it.)

The fault lies, I think, with much of the terminology and with the way in which function is described. People are asked to serve on campaign committees instead of joining a group to help solve some relevant and urgent problem. They are asked "to take a few names," with such a palpable effort to make the task sound easy that the end effect is to make it seem trivial and of no great importance either way. The trouble is, you see, that fund-raising is put ahead of program, instead of the other way around. And there is nothing there at all to appeal to pride of association or a responsible concern for the continuity.

Father John E. Walsh, vice-president for academic affairs at the University of Notre Dame, gets to the root of the enlistment problem when he reminds us, "Aristotle pointed out long ago [that] the finest compliment one man can ever pay another is to ask him to do a favor." And another pertinent suggestion, certainly at the top level of the problem, is not to ask people to join a committee, but to point out—if it is true—that they are in fact part of the local power structure and that this is a situation in which the power structure has a responsible job to do, or otherwise the job just won't get done.

Causes don't need "workers" so much as they need

"informed and dedicated advocates." And we should know by this time that these are the people who have become involved in program, who have already committed themselves by word, deed, and gift, who know the story best and feel most deeply about it.

"Training workers" is a hardy perennial, always gracing the conference agenda but seldom getting very far. There is much talk of indoctrination, and my Jewish colleagues tell me that their workers are rarely allowed to take assignments without having first attended at least one or two indoctrination meetings. But the fault even there is the very attempt to produce instant advocacy, with expert monologue flogging away at the captive audience but with little or no involvement in program, building up genuine pride of association, or achieving some degree of personal identification by dialogue and guided discussion. Daniel Willard, years ago the great president of the Baltimore & Ohio Railroad, once said to me, when I was working with him in his other role as trustee chairman for Johns Hopkins University, that if all you want is alfalfa, you can have three crops a year, but that if you want an oak tree, you have to allow more time. This may be what made me think of my own line, two decades later, that you can't make a good pickle just by squirting vinegar on a cucumber—it has to soak awhile.

Quantitatively, the traditional requirement is ten workers to each captain. But the common practice today is moving toward the simpler formula of one worker for every five prospects and a captain for every five workers. And despite all that has been said about worker imperfection, let's not sneer at the idea of mere numbers. All the old studies have shown that there is a direct relationship between the number of workers and the final amount of the money raised. However it may be done, the more workers there are, the more money you will get.

Finally, in considering this general problem of organization, planners should give another thought to terminology. The word "commission" may be better for your purposes than "committee." And if there is a semblance of genuine continuity in what you propose to do, such as a standing committee for development work, the word "board" has advantages. Moreover, in the early stages of enlistment—particularly where institutional loyalties have little or no bearing and where the defense mechanisms of prospective workers may be easily triggered—it is sometimes well to avoid altogether the usual terms of formal organization. Anyhow, whatever the semantics, it seems reasonable to conclude that volunteers are no more to be lured by the talk and techniques of organization charts than brides-to-be can be enticed by talk of dishpans. So watch your language, brothers; watch your language.

If there is an art here, it is more an art of public relations than anything else, involving pride, recognition, optimism, universality, and dramatization. And the higher you hold your standards, the better people will perform. But let's always be fair about it, remembering that the best of the volunteers always have the inescapable limitations of diversity of interest, limited attention periods, and secondary responsibility. These three factors should never be overlooked in your planning and never forgotten while the show goes on.

Meetings and Planned Events

It is a standard posture of many insiders, and of veteran workers too, that for them campaign meetings are unnecessary; they know all they need to know, they claim, and can spend their time to better advantage in some other way.

They are wrong. For there are many sound reasons why all group movements need the dynamics of meetings and planned events—from start to finish and at whatever places and intervals may be needed to sustain interest and momentum.

In Carl Kersting's phrase, you need meetings as "a series of serious deadlines"—dates against which you can press for action, set intermediate goals, and aim for fresh targets just ahead.

You need too the dialogue and the discussion. As I said many years ago, indirect communication has its proper function, but the best business is always done by putting a lot of feet under tables and letting the gums beat.

Also, the good worker goes to meetings for one of the reasons he goes to church—to bear witness. He gains, and the cause gains, because he is seen, is greeted, and by the very osmosis of fellowship grows in his stature, his competence, and his faith.

Other good reasons are that meetings yield publicity and thus create sustained visibility for the cause, and under the right conditions can make for useful competition, good training for future workers, and a sense of enthusiastic unity for everybody. As any one of the many Ringling brothers would have told you, there's nothing like a bandwagon.

Many chest meetings, good models because there are so many of them, with such varied experience, are run with music, trophies, and almost a carnival atmosphere—in a light spirit, with fun for all as well as public measurement of organized activity. The best of these meetings are so good, and so effective afterward as community conversation pieces, that many local business houses gladly compete to act as hosts, pick up the tab, and thus help keep campaign costs down.

All meetings need sharp timing. The first in any series of meetings should start right on time, regardless of how many are tardy, and finish on time as previously advertised. Otherwise the contagion of tardiness will delay all successive meetings by sadly increasing margins. Grand Rapids, years ago, found it useful to run a preluncheon meeting for leaders at 11:30 A.M. and call the regular report meeting at exactly 12:07 P.M. instead of 12 or 12:30. They all got there on time, and they all probably set their watches every morning.

How many meetings to have varies, of course, with the circumstances. Fast local campaigns often have report meetings every day. National causes rarely get everybody together more than once or twice a year. There has to be enough time to let the workers do some work but not enough to let them slow down. It is having to get up there and report and face your fellow workers that keeps Sammy running.

Discussion and review are of the essence. So the presiding officer should always throw questions around, work hard for audience participation generally, and summarize at every appropriate opportunity—especially before adjournment. Visual aids are helpful, and so is a good written summary of the meeting, sent out as soon afterward as possible to those who were invited but could not attend, with a brief and cheery note attached.

Attendance, incidentally, needs more than formal invitation, which alone is never more than the first blow. Attendance has to be organized, usually table by table. And regardless of the advance count, every meeting should be underset. Even one empty chair makes them wonder who failed to come. But when extra chairs have to be brought in, it tends to make them marvel at the popularity of the cause and the universality and urgency of the appeal.

Sure, there's hokum in some of this, as there has to be with anything needing a slight touch of show business. But perhaps the simplest and soundest explanation is merely to cite the first law of public relations—that actions speak louder than words.

And that explains too why you need planned events—"features," we used to call them—as well as campaign meetings: to dramatize some thought or message, make another hook on which to hang a story, and keep the good talk going. These aims were all served by the parables and by the miracle of the loaves and fishes.

Ask any old pro, and he'll tell you that good meetings and planned events are nothing to be questioned or argued about—you simply have to have them.

Solicitation

This too you have to have, and there are many good ways to explain it. The great Bishop Lawrence of Massachusetts, who raised vast sums more than fifty years ago for the Episcopal Church Pension Fund and to help establish Harvard's Graduate School of Business Administration, used to say that the key to his success was simply "good conversation." Dr. William H. Welch, the incomparable "Popsy" of Johns Hopkins, who personally raised millions of dollars back in the twenties, told me that all he did was to keep talking about what they wanted to do at the Medical School or School of Hygiene and Public Health until he was asked how much it was going to cost.

Austin V. McClain says, "Do not ask for money. Do ask for a better laboratory, a better dormitory, better equip-

ment. . . . Talk about the 'something,' not about money."
My own way of putting it is that nobody ever buys a Buick
just because General Motors needs the money.

All of which, you see, comes down to the same thing:
never ask for money until you have sold the program. And
never tell the donor what to do or how much to give; content yourself always with the expression of hope that he
might give at such and such a level. And then, if you are as
wily a wizard as the old-time gift-procurement men of the
YMCA, you play for the flinch. The man says he will give
$500? And does he say this without flinching? Then comes
the soft suggestion, "For three years?"

It would be well for you to pause right here and review
Chapters 3 and 4. For then it would be easier to understand
the reasons for a few additional bits of advice about the
arts and techniques of solicitation.

It should proceed from the inside out, starting with the
board and the institutional family and then spreading out-
ward, always starting locally with the top group, and always
remembering that fund-raising too is subject to a law of
diminishing returns—the wider the periphery, the greater
the effort, the smaller the gift, and the higher the cost.

Solicitation should also be conducted at the same or higher
level: the solicitor should be a giver whose own giving standards and whose place in the scheme of things are commensurate with the goals he seeks and the people he sees.

At whatever level, the solicitor who picks out his prospects
will raise more money, as a rule, than the solicitor to whom
names have been assigned arbitrarily. And those who have
already given, be it remembered, are always the best prospects.

The order of effectiveness, usually, is face to face, voice to
ear, a genuinely personal letter, and then—away out in left

field—the easy-way methods of appealing by an advertisement, by publicity, and probably last of all, by radio and television. You simply can't get away from personal involvement—if you want thoughtful and proportionate gifts—or away from the fact that about 80 per cent of the people are eye-minded. In mass appeals, "in one ear and out the other" should be taken a lot more literally than you may suppose.

For clinking money, you can shake the can. For folding money, you should go ask for it. But for checks and securities and gifts in pledges, you have to take some pains—make the appointment, perhaps take someone along, count on making two or more calls, and in general give the process enough time and loving care to let it grow and prosper. In the wonderful words of James R. Reynolds, mastermind of the $82-million Program for Harvard College, "No cow will let down her milk in response to a letter or a telephone call. You have got to sit down beside her and go to work."

Most house-to-house solicitation is relatively sterile; the average yield in chest campaigns is less than $5. But there may be program reasons why house-to-house coverage is important, as in the case of the American Cancer Society, whose workers are urged to say, when the front door is opened, "Good afternoon! I have here your copy of cancer's 'Seven Danger Signals.' May I come in?" (Something like this gambit has put the Fuller Brush Co. up where it is, especially when an object is there in the caller's hand, held out to be taken.)

All of the foregoing has to do with the solicitation of individuals. As for foundations and corporations, I have just two pieces of special advice.

One is, don't try to make an end run on the resident almoner by trying to bypass the official setup just because somebody knows an important officer or a member of the board. Auld acquaintance can open doors here, but that's as far as it should go. Anything more just sets up more barriers and stiffens resistance.

The other advice is that solicitation in these two special areas is not for laymen or volunteers, but is best done by the "expert witness"—some top man or woman who is directly involved in the program to be discussed and has all the right answers for the expert questions. Even trustees, and sometimes especially trustees, are a doubtful choice for these assignments—assuming, as we increasingly must, that the persons to be called upon are knowledgeable professionals on the giving side of the fence.

Finally, Princeton's Mr. Oates, who could be quoted to good effect all the way from here to there, has this manna in miniature for all solicitors:

> You need the numbers to get the few that count most; first, to uncover the unknowns, and thus find the "miracle gifts," and second, because the big givers simply won't give without evidence that run of mine givers "are excited into giving."
>
> Push hard for high standards, but accept gracefully the donor's ultimate decision. . . . Most of all you need faith. And for faith you must believe that failure is unthinkable.

Timing

The two most important things to bear in mind about timing are that whatever anyone has plenty of time to do is what rarely gets done, and that if you wait for just the right time to launch your fund-raising campaign, it will never get off the ground.

In any campaign, it pays to say again, you have to press for planned accomplishment within calculated deadlines.

The minimum timing, usually, for annual and purely local campaigns, such as chest and united funds and every-member canvasses in churches, is about ten days, to cover two weekends. The big capital campaigns, with virtually national coverage, are now taking about three years, allowing in any case for three tax years for the collection of pledges.[9] This also, be it noted, allows enough time for the original contributors to clear the decks for their second contributions. (Of the last $20 million given to Harvard College, $15 million was in repeat gifts in the vital last six months of the campaign starting on February 13, 1957, and ending on January 20, 1960.)

Momentum

Akin to timing is the perennial and difficult problem, more peculiar to capital campaigns, of sustaining momentum—of keeping alive and vibrant the feeling that the cause is relevant, important, and urgent.

To be casual in any courtship may possibly win the meager victory of casual consent. Anything like warmly enthusiastic compliance, however, requires bringing to bear all the good dynamics that can be summoned. Some people deplore pressure, but nothing worthwhile ever gets done without it. Charles W. Eliot knew this when he said, "Now press you on," and Harvard liked his words so well that it made them the title of a major campaign pamphlet.

Momentum has to be the special responsibility of the leadership, but nowhere does staff or professional skill mean more. No other reason is so accountable for program and campaign failure. For while men have learned to cope with accident and disaster, no easy cure has ever been found for indifference and apathy.

Information alone is no specific. Accents on slumps and cries of crisis get more yawns than tears. Sometimes tandem leadership helps, with the fresh voice and face of a new chairman following the original leadership, and by original design. Most often, however, the best insurance is planned action with the emphasis on optimism and universality, coupled always with the consistent and undaunted stand for victory taken and held by the institution's top man.

Slumps are inevitable in fund-raising, just as they are in baseball. The turn for the better comes soonest to those who stand up there uncomplainingly and keep swinging hard.

Communication and Publicity

Continuity is the big thing here, rather than the snow job that tries to overwhelm everybody by sheer variety and volume. Information alone, as the National Safety Council has found, yields little or no action; and publicity alone, it is worth repeating, raises little or no money.

Publicity does set the stage, state the message, and lets everybody know from time to time that our flag is still there. But publicity, out of the necessities of competition and cost if nothing else, is constantly becoming more selective, and tailor-made for special tasks and special situations. Its four chief roles in fund-raising today, I think, are announcement, general explanation, reporting on events and campaign progress, and, with rising importance, providing conversation pieces for organized advocates—not for mailing, but to be taken along on personal calls.

Campaign pamphlets were discussed in Chapter 4 (page 44). So at this point may I merely summarize a few bits of special advice:

People skim more than they read. So keep it short and keep it simple.

Whatever it is, make it easy to read, with short sentences and short paragraphs. (Those four-letter words have tended to get a bad name, and that's a great pity, for nowhere in our rich and colorful language is there to be found greater punch and persuasion.)

For continuity and momentum and for sustaining confidence, there is nothing better than a terse and cheery bulletin, probably 8½ by 11 in size and no more than four pages. These can carry the news, create the mood, give the varied testimony, pay the tributes, and offer the priceless nuggets of program information.

Tax leaflets are nice to have, if only to make the workers feel better. But they needn't be long. In fact, some of the best have been reduced to a simple card. (The Annual Giving Office at Princeton has just such a card, size 3⅜ by 8, fitting either a pocket or a #10 envelope.)

If there must be much variety in the literature, a sure-fire device both to improve attention and to forestall criticism of printing expenditures is the "tent," or "hanger"— a small piece of paper to be folded over the top of the front cover, explaining why this particular piece was sent to this particular person. (Some add teasers, such as "See pp. 3 and 7," or "Mr. Doakes says to tell you he's sure you'll want to study this carefully.")

If you must have a slogan, search out something with the best personal identification. The best slogan I ever heard of, for instance, was used in Dayton when they ran a campaign to repair the ravages of the 1913 flood: "Remember what you promised when you were up in the attic."

Speakers can always use a handbook or data sheets, but few speakers relish obviously canned talks. Some of the best speakers are those who in effect are beneficiaries of the cause, such as teachers and students. And sometimes the best speakers of all are the very young, who can warm the heart, moisten the eye, and make Walter Mittys out of everybody there. (As in church, no matter who the speaker, no souls are saved after fifteen or twenty minutes.)

Designers should have fun, and trade medals at the professional meetings for their cute and clever ideas. But the really good ones never forget that their best audiences are bifocal and allergic to strange effects and to change.

Radio programs and motion pictures will not be discussed here. Their cost mounts, and much time is involved. Whether they ever pay out I just don't know.

Finally, it strikes one more blow for dialogue versus monologue to quote Mr. Oates again. He says the best medium of communication in the big Princeton campaign was the long-distance telephone.

He was referring here especially to the organized telephone solicitation of alumni during the general canvass and cleanup stages of the campaign. This has been done at a number of institutions, both in annual giving and in capital campaigns. And the way it was done at Princeton in the spring and fall of 1961 has been described for you with color and clarity by Edgar M. Gemmell, now a consultant and for many years the top promotional man as Princeton's administrative vice-president:

> We set up a telephone room in Nassau Hall, with half a dozen instruments. And we insisted on that location because we thought it was important to have the calls come from the one building which best of all symbolized the institution.
>
> All day and well into the evening we had volunteers, class by class, phoning their classmates; letting them hear all those bells and boiler-room noises, and going through a routine which went something like this:

"Fred? Hi there, boy, it's Joe!" "Joe? Why, where the hell are you calling from? Aren't you still in Cleveland?" "Yeah, I still live in Cleveland, but right now I'm here in Nassau Hall, with Charlie and Shorty and old Bug-Eye. And we're calling the class to tell them about the big thing going on here at Princeton. . . ."

No BIG dough this way, but it sold a lot of potatoes; single thousands, fives, tens, and a few gifts in six figures.

And now, if you remember what was said in Chapter 1 about people, the two big reasons for this success will stand right out: the universal desire to be sought and the equally universal need to be a worthwhile member of a worthwhile group. It was personal, it was all on the same or higher level, and everybody had fun. And you just can't beat that combination.

Reports

There is no trouble about oral reports at meetings, except with the classic drone who rises blandly to repeat that his peerless crew is still "just getting organized." But there is always plenty of trouble in getting written reports, especially field reports in national or regional campaigns, with enough objectivity to yield the solid facts headquarters needs to know.

Who was seen, and what did they agree to do, and by what time? What happened that particular week, in terms of recruiting, solicitation, gifts, meetings, etc.? What is the field man going to do next, and where? These are samples of the real meat, and it is hard to get. Even now, many years later, I can feel my own neck hairs rise at the reports one man used to make: "Attitude here highly favorable," "Things in this area in good shape," and other similar gems signifying exactly nothing.

Like the old-time blacksmith fashioning a horseshoe, all you can do is just keep banging away. Insist on regularity at a mimimum of weekly intervals, reject the meaningless generalities, and keep ever at the quest for facts.

You there at the controls are not the only one to whom the reports are vital. For reports ensure action. He who must report must have something to say. So he almost has to do something.

And one more thing to remember about reports, including your own. All campaigns, some of us were trained to believe, should have a written history, with a detailed chronology—if only for the sake of others who must follow and for answering the inevitable questions of comparable institutions. The better your report file and the records kept daily and weekly, the easier it will be to write a meaningful final report.

Receipt and Acknowledgment

Checks and securities may have to linger a few days, but receipts should go out fast. The giver wants the acknowledgment, and the worker wants the information. More will be said about this in Chapter 6, under "Rewards and Recognition." Right here the thing to note is that the system for posting and receipt must be all set up and ready to go from the very start.

Mail Appeals

Even in organized fund-raising there is a place for mail appeals. Most alumni funds center their methods on class-agent letters.[10]And in New York City, for example, almost all the local campaigns—hundreds of them every year—lean heavily on appeals by mail. And of course even in well-managed capital campaigns the job has to be done by mail wherever the prospects are too few, or rated too low, to justify the visitation required for organized committee work.

So what's the good word here?

Francis Pray, former vice-president of the Council for Financial Aid to Education, put it nicely when he said campaign letters should be "love letters," seeking "to marshal winning words to convince the recipient of our regard for him and our need and desire for his regard for us and his support for our enterprises."

This is right in line with what was said in Chapter 1 about people: that we all want to be sought and want to be worthwhile members of a worthwhile group. So Mr. Pray's words are a fresh way to express what we all like to keep repeating: namely, that letters should be personalized in every possible way and never considered as something preferable to personal contact or as just another project in mass communication—faceless, anonymous, generalized, and probably futile.

The signer, therefore, should always review his list and check the names needing personal salutations, personal signatures (first name only and sometimes nicknames), and possibly personal postscripts—which incidentally should always have top billing as the place in the letter most apt to get attention. It is for this basic reason of personal identification that multiple signatures and signings by national figures or Hollywood personalities have no place. And many times it is better to use the signer's own personal or business stationery, rather than the campaign letterhead of the cause itself.

The copy should look and read like a letter and not like an editorial. And the right sequence is still the classic order of attention, interest, confidence, desire, and action—hopefully with the P.S. reserved for the best medicine of all, what the signer of the letter has done about all this himself.

Enclosures should be brief and simple—usually a subscription blank with some terse sales copy of its own, together with a pocket-size leaflet designed to back up the letter's message and to stress the angles of universality and thoughtful giving.

All mail appeals should have at least one follow-up letter —never with any implication of reproach because the first letter went unanswered, but rather with news of developments since the first mailing, reports on gifts others have made, and anything else that has a chance of arousing interest, creating confidence, and getting action.

The timing, if possible, should tie in with current publicity and with delivery on Tuesday, Wednesday, or Thursday. (The Salvation Army often delays the mailing of its Christmas letters until the weather turns bad, preferably with a heavy snow or even a nice blizzard, and likes to defer its appeals for summer camps until some June day when it's hotter than hot.)

Vary the format with underlined words and indented paragraphs. Stress the note of urgency with some reasonable or plausible deadline. And whatever else you do, finish the letter with a last paragraph that asks for something specific, preferably in terms of program. (Will you send that kid to camp for a week?)

There are many good books on the use of direct mail, with many more details than these. My own last word would be this: use the mail for supplementary purposes, rather than as an evasion of organized personal contact, and make the letters as personal as they can be. The test should be, as in many good alumni funds, whether the approach is customary and expected and at a level on which the influence is at its best.

Cleanup Campaigns

Whatever the result, even with full victory, every campaign winds up with unfinished business. And the one important thing to say about cleanup efforts is that they should always be planned *in advance*. Improvised measures seldom work and often cause more mischievous alarm than constructive activity. Whereas the advance planning, with special leadership and workers recruited weeks ahead, tends to beget confidence and optimism. "We planned it that way" is good medicine in fund-raising too.

Costs

You can't raise money without spending money, and within reasonable limits the return is likely to be commensurate with the investment.

With costs always rising, for postage, printing, paper, salaries and travel, smart help becomes more and more important, and so does hard work on the campaign budget—a sample for the items of which is shown here. The thing to do in making this budget is to figure out what the costs are apt to be for what the plan says you should do, in terms of staff, tools, facilities, and time. And whatever you do, avoid jumping to conclusions about what the percentage cost should be, either as a matter of someone's opinion or on the basis of what the percentage cost turned out to be in some comparable but completed campaign. In the latter case, be sure the comparison is based on similar data, especially in the charges for rent, charges against the payroll account, and charges for other items, like report luncheons, for which others may have picked up the tab.

In all campaigns, the cost will vary with scope, time, and size of goal, and most of the cost will usually be involved in

CHECK LIST FOR CAMPAIGN BUDGET

1. *Salaries and Fees*
   a. Professional staff
   b. Clerical
   c. Federal deductions
   d. Fees for professional firm, auditors, etc.

2. *Organization Expense*
   a. Luncheons, dinners and meetings
   b. Travel *

3. *Promotion and Publicity*
   a. Printed material
   b. Art work
   c. Models and visualizations
   d. Direct-mail costs
   e. Stills and motion pictures
   f. Special-presentation expense
   g. Radio and TV

4. *General Expense*
   a. Rent
   b. Furniture and fixtures
   c. Business machines
   d. Office supplies
   e. Telephone and telegraph †
   f. Postage
   g. Freight and express
   h. Messenger service
   i. Electricity and water
   j. Service and repairs
   k. Insurance
   l. Bank charges and interest

5. *Contingencies*

* To ensure representative attendance at meetings in national campaigns, the travel expenses of volunteers in excess of $50 are often charged here.

† May include charges for long-lines hookups at simultaneous meetings in important cities.

raising the last 10 per cent of the money. Annual campaigns run for less than 10 or 15 per cent have all the cost respectability anyone has a right to expect and in some communities perhaps a touch of uniqueness. Capital campaigns might go as high as that when the goals are low, but the big ones often keep their costs well below 5 per cent.[11]

People seldom ask about costs, and it is a poor practice to raise the subject by bragging about how low your costs are. More often than not, you are probably spending too little. And that suggests closing these few paragraphs about costs by quoting once more the good Mr. Oates:

"With good management and planning," he says, "the expenses will be meaningless." Nevertheless, every campaign should have a budget, and the preceding check list will show you the items usually included. *General note:* Campaign costs are rising steadily. Some of the larger campaigns start now with a provisional budget only. All budgets should be based on actual planning, rather than arbitrary percentages, and should be subject to revision at sensible intervals. They should be regarded primarily as an essential adjunct of planning, and as a useful check on management.

The Never-Never or Hardly-Ever Country

And now let's have a brief look at some bad or questionable techniques and at two of our mossiest myths. (See accompanying "Seven Deadly Sins of Fund-Raising.")

First, because the very idea is so irksome to all good pros and so flagrantly contrary to their codes, may I say that no ethical or reputable fund-raising firm does business on a percentage basis. All twenty-eight members of the American Association of Fund-Raising Counsel have been pledged against that practice ever since the association was founded

SEVEN DEADLY SINS OF FUND-RAISING

1. *Ad-libbing.* No study, no planning, no preparation, no consultation, no concurrence, and hence no organized and unified agreement.

2. *Panhandling.* Asking for support merely because you need the money. No explanation; hence no motivation for thoughtful and proportionate giving.

    ("Any amount will be welcome" cheapens the cause and beggars the giver by putting fund-raising ahead of program.)

3. *Automation.* Human equation gives way to mechanics, with role of voluntary mission abdicated to the postman and publicist.

4. *Groupism.* Opposite of universality—undemocratic, divisive, and sterile.

    (No single group can organize a community.)

5. *Averaging.* Accent on averages leads to lower standards—in leadership, volunteer participation, and levels of giving.

6. *Pessimism.* Only genuine emergencies can make fund-raising assets out of gloom and despair. More often than not we aim too low and plead rather than challenge.

    (Whenever you let them know it isn't going well, the chances are everything will stop right there.)

7. *Parsimony.* The good omelet needs enough broken eggs. More often than not, fund-raising costs are set too low.

back in 1935. Even before that (and certainly today) their charges were on a fee basis, graduated according to the number of men assigned, the expense involved, and duration of their service.[12, 13]

Considered questionable by chests, Better Business Bureaus, and the National Information Bureau are all schemes to raise money by "Remit or return" for unsolicited merchandise. You may ignore such stuff or chuck it out, and you'll be breaking no law.

You don't see many "tag days" any more, and you may be sure that can-shaking and coin boxes are more for worker satisfaction and sheer visibility than for raising significant sums of money. The Salvation Army dispensed with "Mercy Boxes" many years ago, despite the social-work angle that the collection process gave work to some older men, simply because the total cost exceeded the income.

Lotteries of one kind or another get envious mention now and then, especially since staid New Hampshire voted for them. But John S. Knight, head of the Knight newspapers, had what I thought was the best word on this when he said, on March 15, 1964, "A lottery may be a 'painless' way of raising money. It can also lead to corruption and destroy an individual's sense of obligation."

Benefits are like raisins in rice pudding: many people like them. They do take the time and talents of a lot of fine women and do give the agency or cause involved a welcome amount of newspaper publicity. Perhaps they may lead some people to become interested in agency program and even to make special gifts and bequests. But grant all this and more, and the fact remains that benefits do little or nothing for thoughtful and proportionate giving, and almost always are run at shockingly high cost. Fifty per cent is more usual than rare, and many have costs that run higher than that. But it is the return in light of the effort that is beginning to trouble the more thoughtful fund-raisers. That is probably why the Lutheran Church is reported to have taken an open stand against church suppers and why the Massachusetts Council of Churches believes "bazaar workers could find better things to do with their time."

One of our most universal and persistent myths is that the way to raise money is by the multiplication table. I remember a time in Garden City years ago, among a group that wanted to raise $500,000 to build a memorial airport on Long Island to honor General "Billy" Mitchell, when some resident genius arose to suggest that the easiest way to do this was to get a million people in that area to give 50 cents each. And I can assure you that no pro has won his spurs until he has heard at least five good men and true propose at various times that the best way to raise $1 million is to get 1,000 men to give $1,000—just as simply as that.

"Buck a month" clubs, popular out on the Coast in World War II, were merely another variation of the same Euclidean idea, and I must say that the public's understanding of the fallacy in such reasoning has not been helped by the so-called "March of Dimes." Far too many people, I suppose, think that dimes actually did the trick; whereas if every living soul in the United States had given a dime to the National Foundation for Infantile Paralysis, as it was called in pre-Salk days, the total raised that way could never have equaled, or come anywhere near equaling, the foundation's poorest year in fund-raising.

Let us safely conclude, in these remarks about the fatal charms of the multiplication table, that it will always be well to eschew a quest for quarters almost as assiduously as a campaign to collect $3 bills.

The other big myth is what I have long called "the William Jennings Bryan complex." This is getting to be ancient history, with only 23 per cent of those now living able to recall anything about World War I. But one of the best stories of that time, for our purposes here, is about what the great commoner had to say when Theodore Roosevelt and Gen. Leonard Wood first proposed a special camp at Plattsburg, New York, for the training of officers and the advancement of our military preparedness. Bryan, then the somewhat disastrous Secretary of State under Woodrow Wilson, thundered his sonorous objections on the ground that valiant Americans needed no such preparation. "For if any foreign foe should ever threaten our fair shores," he cried, "a million men would spring to arms overnight." Bryan never realized, you see, that spontaneity works best when it is well planned. And for all his Bible lecturing, he never stopped to think, apparently, that it wasn't raining when Noah started building the ark.

And then the days of 1935, unknown now to 47 per cent of our people, gave us the lesson of the Will Rogers Memorial. Will Rogers had lost his life on a round-the-world flight with Wiley Post, and many of his most powerful friends sought to honor his memory by a fund with no goal or program, but one in which they would open the floodgates of publicity, make it as easy as possible to contribute by posting signs inviting subscriptions in all bank teller windows and in all post offices, and then let the people do the rest. And there were state chairmen in forty-seven states and 2,732 local chairmen. And except for the nonexistent television, nobody has ever seen such complete and daily publicity. The "drive" opened in September, and was supposed to close on Thanksgiving Day. But on December 14, 1935, after an extension, there were 105,176 givers on the books, and the best anyone could say was that it was hoped the total would eventually come to at least $300,000. But the total that day, from all those people, was $65,802.72—with campaign expenses, despite all the free service and donated space, of $59,716.92.

There were two lessons there. One was that memorial campaigns hardly ever get gifts that would do any more than buy some flowers unless the program phase of the memorial is big and strong. And the other is that publicity alone raises little or no money, especially without program, without goals and quotas, without open standards for giving, and without commitment, coverage, and conversation.

Finally, in this review of some of the don't's in fund-raising, may I say what I'm sure many believe to be true, that the commonest threats and errors are in the area of semantics. Words, just words.

Nearly everyone, I suppose, still refers to institutions like Amherst, Brown, Harvard, Yale, and Princeton, and to similar institutions clear across to Leland Stanford, as "privately endowed" whereas the connotations of those two words are about as unfairly misleading as they can be. Actually, they are independent rather than private, and they are gift-supported to a far greater extent than endowed.

Causes, whenever possible, should be identified with the program rather than with the means for financing it. "United Community Services," therefore, makes more sense to me than "United Community Fund." For whether it's a car or an automatic dishwasher, most people are interested in what a gadget looks like and what it does, and couldn't care less about what makes it go. So why do we put so much public emphasis on fund-raising machinery?

The same principle applies to the enlistment of workers. But where our semantics really go haywire is in the language of solicitation—the "language of request," as

David McCord put it so gracefully. For here the poison is to talk of cards and averages and to assure the prospective donor that "any amount will be welcome, no matter how small."

Still, even that is not quite as lethal as that good old line, "Sorry I can't work, but I'll be glad to lend my name."

All of which, I think, strongly supports the thesis of my old friend Carlton G. Ketchum, president of Ketchum, Inc., who says, "The basic concern of fund-raising is not money: it is people. . . . It demands an intuitive sense about people, and a spiritual sense of the goodness of life." And that means the careful employment of thought, good planning, and loving care.

SUMMARY

I hope you yourself, after going through all these pages of Chapter 5, may have reached a few conclusions like these:

1. Effective fund-raising is never easy, but it can always be simple: get the dedicated advocates committed by their own words, deeds, and gifts; organize to achieve reasonable coverage; then aim all your promotion, in an atmosphere of pride and responsible concern for the continuity, toward the arts of good conversation.

2. All campaigns should create and sustain the mood of relevance, importance, and urgency, with an attitude of faith and confidence.

3. Program should always be kept ahead of fund-raising in everything planned and all you do. Sell the opportunities and not the deficiencies, never forgetting that money flows to promising programs and not to needy institutions.

4. Every good campaign is essentially a public relations operation—an aggregate of the tremendous trifles by which

any enterprise wins and holds public approval: good manners, pleasurable experiences, recognition for achievement, and proof that all the sacrifice anyone made was worth far more than it cost.

5. And never fear pressure. Seek it out and use it in full and cheerful measure. Without its leverage, in terms of quotas and deadlines, nothing will move, and your campaign will languish and die.

6. Perhaps above all, give every step a plan and every move a timing. And if all else goes blank, just remember that the essence of it all is that somebody, with some good reasons, has to see somebody about giving some money for the advancement of some good cause.

And now let's see what there is to do after your campaign has been happily concluded.

Chapter 6

Postcampaign Goals and Programs

*Y*our fund-raising campaign has ended. Many decisions are then to be made, and many moves. But even deciding just when the end should be is in itself a momentous and complicated matter, sometimes beyond control and always worthy of good thought and planning.

The end is not necessarily when the dollar goal has been made, nor can the end always be deferred successfully because the goal is still out of reach. About the only general conclusion one may prudently draw, in fact, is that there is one set of rules for annual campaigns and another for campaigns for capital.

In annual campaigns, the best and most common practice

is to hold fast to the concluding date established and publicized at the very beginning. On that date, so far as dollars are concerned, the books are closed—though it is a common practice in chest campaigns to "anticipate" certain gifts not in but considered safe, in fixing the total on closing day. Moreover, some of the best of the alumni funds hold open the roll of donors for as long as another thirty days.

These practices maintain the validity of the deadline for both working and giving and thus preserve a hard rule without which all future efforts would be gravely compromised. For, as many smaller community chests and united funds have found too late for correction, whenever a constituency of any kind gets accustomed to deferment and delay, the pattern of discouragement and defeat tends to become fixed.

And yet no peril has been found in the secondary practice of keeping the donor rolls open for a reasonable time. To be sure, there is more face than fund in this—sensible and understandable satisfactions for both workers and givers. But the fund also prospers, when the dollar goal has been reached, by putting the postcampaign money aside as a nucleus for the following year.

But suppose the annual campaign has fallen short of its goal. In that case, there should be only two alternatives.

One is to announce the final result, with little or no public reference to the original goal, and open comparison with the previous year only if that result has now been excelled. Any additional fund-raising should then be done quietly and more as cleanup than as extended campaign. (Except for the disappointment of the leaders, this won't hurt as much as you might think. For the public's memory for goals and such is always and everywhere mercifully short.)

At closing time in such cases, plus factors should be pointed out, and especially any increase in the number of contributors or the number of volunteer workers. But all hosannas should be measured with taste and care and addressed primarily to those who actually deserve them. Play up such people, and give them prizes and public esteem. But never risk public confidence or cheapen the recognition of those who have really labored in the vineyard by indiscriminate hymns of praise for the "hard work and sacrifice" of those whose efforts, if any, are notorious for having been trivial and fruitless.

The alternative, if the additional dollars are of real and paramount importance, is to proceed as indicated above, but to organize a new and special fund-raising apparatus—with a name and goal all its own and all the power-structure type of personnel that can be mustered. For this in itself, whatever the result in dollars, will serve public notice, far better than the lamentations of the defeated leadership could possibly do, that the program is vital, that the goal has validity, and that men of stature and influence are behind the cause. Change of pace and change of approach are the vital factors here, if the extended effort is to win confidence and establish more plausibly an image of relevance, importance, and urgency. Incidentally—it should hardly need to be said at this point—the best place to look for the additional money is among those who have already given—not nominally, but thoughtfully and proportionately. Best source of all: the hard-working advocates among the top givers.

With either of these two alternatives, be it noted, the formal end of any annual campaign should be held to the original date. For to do otherwise is always to set habit patterns that mortgage the future and handcuff succeeding leadership. Fund-raising management in these situations, I have always felt, has a serious and often difficult responsibility for insistently reminding the temporary lay leadership that annual campaigns are repeat business, that improvised measures with roots in defeat are almost certain to fail, and that all plans for the cleanup should be made well in advance.

Now in capital campaigns, deciding when the end should be is quite another dish of tea.

We start here with the dictum that the higher the goal and the broader the scope, the more time will be needed. It is also common practice now to let the established campaign period cover at least three taxable years so as to make the most of the pledge factor and to allow enough time for the original donors to make repeat gifts[14]—which they often do of their own accord. But there is a nice and delicate point here: allowing enough time but not so much as to invite procrastination and thus defer action. Here as in all human affairs, the inertia problem is always bad enough without encouraging it.

The closing date in capital campaigns has an importance of its own as the ultimate pressure point, though always preceded by enough intermediate climax dates to keep things moving. And then it is, when the original date nears, that the time comes to decide when the campaign will really come to an end.

As a practical matter, this will hardly ever be on the original closing date, if only for the simple reason, whether or not the dollar goal has been reached, that there are always a number of important solicitations still hanging fire. And this means, nine times out of ten, a special plan for the homestretch—usually with fresh leadership and special workers recruited among those who did best in the formal campaign period. Whether the rest of the unraised money in the original goal should be tucked in with other needs to make a new goal, with fresh identification, is a question that depends first on the size of the problem but most of all on how much steam there is in the barrel. Certainly the trumpet should never blow with uncertain sound. Optimism and universality should be the order of the day, and triumph the song for all. Only pride can win, and pity for failure will get you simply nothing at all.

And so, whenever the end and whatever the type of campaign, it now becomes in order to review the suggested agenda for the postcampaign aims and programs. I have eight topics here, approximately in the order in which they should be considered: loose ends, evaluation and records, rewards and recognition, ensuring the continuity, repairs and replacements, changing the targets, reappraisal of needs, and pledge collections.

Loose Ends

One of the inevitabilities in this always imperfect world is those loose ends—the big and little bits of unfinished business. There are letters to be written, accounts to be closed, furniture and equipment to be sold, returned, or transferred, employees to be paid off—and in some cases other jobs to be found for them—and just a lot of that and this and those.

Principally, all solicitations still hanging fire even after the cleanup period need fresh study, one by one, as do the cases of those who said they couldn't give during the campaign but would do so later. Some names like these need reassignment, either because the worker is exhausted or because the worker and the prospect are not on the right terms. Some situations need cancellation, but all need hand-tailored attention, and the sooner the better. For at this stage death on the vine comes quickly.

Whatever the loose ends may be, they should be listed,

assigned with deadlines, and pursued with cheerful vigor toward their final disposition. Cleaning them up swiftly is not mere tidiness, nice as that is. It is important as good public relations and fruitful as fund-raising.

Evaluation and Records

Another postcampaign job on which no time should be lost is the vital process of evaluation and records.

While the campaign staff is still on the job, and preferably with lay participation by an informal group or a special committee, a meeting should be called for evaluation and recommendations for the future.

What was good, and what was fruitless? What expenses were most worthwhile, and where was expense money relatively wasted or ineffective? What publicity measures were actually productive? Which pieces of literature were most useful to the workers, which pieces pulled best, and which were weak or won the least attention? What kind of meetings were most valuable, and at what places and times of the day? What types of solicitation got the most gifts and the highest responses? What was done that doubtless should be repeated, and what was there that should forever be abandoned? What younger people should be kept in mind and moved up to higher places, who showed the best promise for future leadership?

Right down the line, while no face is to be lost and memories are fresh, this task of evaluation and consensus should be done promptly and thoroughly. It's fun, actually, but someone will have to push, or the job won't get done. Too many voices, let me warn you, will make the plaintive cry that everybody is just too tired.

Coupled with evaluation, because the two tasks cross at so

many places, is the job of making the record, usually as a formal final report on the campaign. This makes welcome reading for those who worked on the campaign, is invaluable for future reference, and will be frequently sought by similar causes and sister institutions.

For annual campaigns, such reports are usually brief and more statistical than subjective—though if you want to see how entertaining such a report can be, you should see how Elliot Jensen does it every year for the United Appeal of Greater Cleveland. For capital campaigns, the content and the length should be suited to the situation. Those who make hard work of it end up with something pretty dull. But when the aim is really illumination, brightness always comes through. And of all such recent reports on capital campaigns I have seen, the best were Harvard's and Princeton's.

Brief or extensive, the record should give the findings of evaluation, figures for the varying sizes and numbers of gifts sought and obtained, a list of the materials used, with quantities, a final budget report on campaign expenses, and a chronology showing the timing of the principal announcements and campaign events. Brief statements on the origins of the effort and the policies pursued could also be useful in most instances. But all reports and records, as a bare minimum, should show the goals, the results, and the timing.

Rewards and Recognition

As already noted, people respond to rewards and recognition somewhat like performing seals and white mice. Certainly no part of the postcampaign procedure can be much more important.

Letters of thanks both to workers and givers have been standard practice for a long time. But tasteful differentiation has been brought to bear in more recent years—suiting the measurement of gratitude to fit the deed, just as Gilbert's Mikado sought to let the punishment fit the crime. Really significant achievement, either in working or giving, customarily gets the full treatment—letters from the campaign chairman, the president of the institution, and even heads of affected departments. (When the late John D. Rockefeller, Jr. gave $4 million to Brown University as his final gift to alma mater and his final tribute to Henry M. Wriston, the retiring president, some of his classmates wrote him "Johnny Rock" letters—and they were really wonderful.)

Such letters are important in themselves, but even more important is setting up a system by which the donors or members of their families will get subsequent reports on what has been accomplished as a result of what they gave. Anniversaries of the original good deed offer pertinent opportunities, as do completion dates on construction, new appointments to endowed professorships, fellowships, and scholarships, important additions to libraries and art collections, and so on. The aim is of course promotional, but the tone should be one of unadorned service—letting the interested person know that his support has had sustained appreciation, and is paying rich dividends. Like all really effective fund-raising, this is in good taste and keeps program out in front where it belongs.

Mementos too are a good device. Cleveland's Jensen, who has been general manager since 1949 and has led that big fund from slightly more than $5 million to more than $14 million, tells me that ornamented cuff links have been awarded there on at least one occasion and that rewards and recognition always play an important role in handing out the halos and putting them where they belong. Yale gave hundreds of special-gifts workers, following the recent capital campaign, a framed etching of the Harkness Tower by Louis Orr, with a brass plate at the bottom, about 2 inches wide, with the simple inscription, "For Service to Yale." This was a tasteful reward, and when hung somewhere in plain sight, made a first-class conversation piece. Harvard gave *The Harvard Book,* a volume of 369 pages with selections by William Bentinck-Smith from three centuries of writings about Harvard—with the following foreword by President Pusey, dated May 15, 1960:

> A Word of Thanks. . . . The present generation of Harvard men, and the generations to come, will always be grateful to the many alumni who gave their time and effort to the Program for Harvard College. This book is given to you as a continuing reminder of the College and a token of her appreciation for your share in the Program's success.

Rewards and recognition for significant service are good business as well as good manners. John Kenneth Galbraith, in *The Scotch,* has this to say about it in his illuminating remarks about leadership:

> Every community needs a great many communal services. To pay for them is expensive; and only a poor class of talent is available for money. By rewarding such work with honor and esteem, the very best men can be had for nothing.

Ensuring the Continuity

In annual campaigns especially, one of the most critical tasks of the postcampaign period is to see that the torch gets passed with a smile. For it comes pretty close to fund-raising homicide when any of the departing brothers get quoted as saying, in effect, "Never again! They'll never catch me on anything like that again—not me!" Damage gets done that way because listeners are seldom aware, as experienced fund-raisers are, that such lamentations usually come from the loafers and laggards, not from those who really worked.

So the prescription for ensuring effective continuity is to make certain the atmosphere is more that of a carnival than a wake—by well-planned high jinks if necessary, but principally by playing up those who are leaving and seeing to it that their message to their successors is one of hope, confidence, and good cheer. Specifically, let me refer again to Mr. Jensen, who says:

> Passing the baton in a happy mood is indeed important. So are honest job descriptions, time schedules, etc., which neither kid nor scare a candidate for leadership. . . . We try hard to give predecessors visibility. Previous trustees become honorary trustees and are urged to attend all meetings. We have a ringside table at campaign meetings for previous officers and leaders. A surprising number keep in touch and are helpful.

Honest job descriptions are indeed important, but I have always felt that in the honeymoon stage of incoming leadership the switch from orange blossoms to dishpans shouldn't be too abrupt. Requests for initial service should begin with something relatively easy; let 'em lick a stamp before you ask 'em to lick an army.

But whatever you do about ensuring the continuity by appreciation, rewards, and recognition, nothing is quite as effective as the convinced and eloquent testimony of a campaign leader who has led a big cause to a great victory. At Buck Hill Falls, Pennsylvania, on May 3, 1962, Princeton's James F. Oates, Jr., told the trustees of the University of Pennsylvania never to let their hearts be troubled about their roles in a big capital campaign:

Of course this is a tough job. It involves lots of work. But it also involves many things like joy and inspiration and fun and rewards beyond measure. . . . You never make better friends than when you're working together for a cause that is greater than you are. . . . You never meet better people than fellow-alumni who join in an effort like this. And I thank the good Lord every day that I had the chance to know scores of Princetonians all over the United States, who wanted this thing to succeed as much as I did, and who were the kind of guys I loved and admired and whom I never would have known as well if this had not been our common experience.

Repairs and Replacements

Like everything else, fund-raising setups need overhauling every once in a while. And there is no better time for it than the postcampaign period.

The list system probably needs to be reviewed, and along with it methods for mailing and distribution. You want all the accuracy you can get, of course, but most of all you want selectivity—clear and complete knowledge of where the power lies and a plan for keeping it informed and active on behalf of your cause. It is an odd but interesting fact that with many institutions this bull's-eye of the continuing target comprises about five hundred names.

Programs for cultivation and club activity and routines for handling speakers and traveling exhibits almost always need a fresh look. Those with experience in national campaigns find out soon enough that it's not such a small world after all and that many a place or region where the cause had been considered reasonably strong will have been proved in campaign tests to have been disappointingly weak and disinterested. Constituency concentrations keep changing, and interests keep moving around and finding new loyalties, to a degree that calls for the best objective scrutiny that can be mustered. Younger men and women, with local standing that is good and on the rise, are believed to be the key here.

New and more effective employment of the "expert witness," among foundations and top corporations especially, will certainly need review. Staff people generally and faculty people in education in particular are bound to have a constantly widening and more critical role to play as the interpretive task becomes narrower and more complicated and as the professional guides to expert giving gain both in sophistication and power. As already found in recent years, student testimony too is increasingly effective, both in formal speaking at meetings and in special roles of personal advocacy.

Publications are often in danger of slipping slowly into multiplication of media, confused purpose, and the mere routine of filling the columns and meeting deadlines. Whatever their traditions—usually their treasured editorial freedom from administrative control—they should be regarded today for what they inevitably have come to be: namely, the voice of the institution. It follows that what they should be saying, and why, ought to have a long and hard look. In all probability, this will bring about some changes.

And then, finally, as you pursue these repairs and replacements, there is always the matter of personnel, complicated in almost all voluntary institutions by our persistently indulgent tolerance for bumbling mediocrity.

The late James R. Angell, after his retirement from the presidency of Yale, told me many years ago that no institution, least of all a great university, could stand universal genius. "The place," he said, "would blow up in less than twenty-four hours." His point, and a good one, was that the routine work of the world has to be done by good but mediocre people. But even the good ones have to be leavened by leadership, or you're lost.

The best vineyards, it has seemed to me, have the right lesson here. The selective process has to be good. The cultivation has to be planned and constant. And the pruning shears need to be kept sharp and ever close at hand. All three of these processes are vital in building and sustaining a sound human framework for fund-raising. Conversely, no cruelty can be much worse than the pity that lets a man stumble along in the wrong job when he might be much happier and more effective somewhere else.

Changing the Targets

Joseph Sweetman Ames, president of Johns Hopkins University more than thirty-five years ago and a physicist of no mean stature, told me two things that have always stuck in my mind. One was that Thomas Young, English physician, physicist, and Egyptologist (1773–1829), was "the last man in the world who knew everything." And the other was why milk stools have three legs: no matter what the terrain, the stool always stands steady. The tripod, Dr. Ames told me, therefore makes the most stable base.

I must suppose that is why the tripod came to my mind some few years ago when I was seeking some simple term for the elements of any development program—annual giving, occasional capital campaigns, and a bequest program. All three types of activity are much in order these days, and can be usefully complementary without being in the least competitive. In fact, any institution that does not have all three legs of this tripod in action simply has an incomplete program. For any one person can give annually, can make an occasional gift for some capital purpose, and can see that his interest in the institution keeps marching on into the future by making a bequest in his will.

The postcampaign procedure here is simply to make sure all three avenues are open, adequately staffed, and properly publicized—that the tripod process is understood and advocated at the top, and has meaning for everybody. The main target will be changed, probably to annual giving—but never, let us hope, to the public exclusion of the two other legs.

Reappraisal of Needs

Just as gratitude is sometimes described as a lively sense of anticipation for favors yet to be received, so it is too that the fulfillment of need is also the birth of fresh desire. With impeccable logic, the strengthened institution finds new muscles, the broader programs seek new frontiers, and the higher standards go looking for loftier perches. As nearly as anything human can be genuinely spontaneous, it may be assumed that almost before the echoes of campaign victory have died away, there will be a new set of institutional needs—often far greater than before.

And this is usually a good thing, for this is surely the stuff of history and the ultimate proof that here is indeed an institution of lively excellence. But here too are new challenge for the involvement of new leadership and, of even more importance, new rationale for the programs of all three legs of the development tripod—partly for increased annual giving, in some degree for the *ad hoc* special-gifts work, and perhaps most of all for the bequest program.

Your concern should be to see that the reappraisal of needs and their arrangement in some order of official priority have the benefit of all the orderly processes of broad participation, with time enough to lay down sound roots and action enough to begin to lay the new foundation of importance, relevance, and urgency. That, you may say, will take you right back to where you should have been in the very beginning. That is true, and it's just fine. For that is exactly where you and your institution ought to be.

One final word on this point, simply because the question seems to come up almost regularly. Waste no time seeking the individual interests of the top layer of your constituency with a view toward breaking the total program into fragments and seeking to match interests with items. The interests are too hard to find anyhow, and they always do better when they evolve of their own accord. Tell the new story in its broad entirety, keep exposing the opportunities in all their bright promise, and then let nature take its course. (As I hope every reader will know by this time, nature may take a little nudging. But that's why you're there, isn't it?)

Pledge Collections

Chests and united funds allow a shrinkage factor of about 4 per cent, not so much because pledges go bad as because people sicken, die, lose their jobs, and move away. Alumni funds, doing a cash business, have no such problems. But sad to say, most churches have the worst collection experience of all annual campaigns, with shrinkages of as much as 10 or 15 per cent all too common. Worst of all, probably, are the telethons; the collection carnage reached 65 per cent in the Bob Hope–Bing Crosby telethon of 1952 for the benefit of the United States Olympic Committee.

In capital campaigns, most of the shrinkage is in the smaller gifts and of no great concern. After the Program for

Harvard College closed on January 20, 1960, cancellations totaled $1,327,719, for a percentage of 1.7. New gifts and pledges after that date more than made up for the loss.

As a practical matter, no institution sues to collect on pledges, except by friendly agreement with some trustee or trust officer for an estate—and often at their request. But all institutions, following capital campaigns, need to have a smooth collection policy and system ready and waiting, with the copy done by the best talent that can be had. Good letters have to be written and sent before any situation that is cooling off has a chance to get stone cold. Fresh proof of the great things being done should always be there, and the more plausible it is made to appear that every dollar is being depended upon, the better the smaller collections will be. Like everything else, the problem needs continuing and first-class attention.

SUMMARY

My hope is that this chapter has made it clear that the postcampaign period is more a time for embracing rich opportunity than a time for complacent convalescence. There is good and happy work to be done, with assurance of solid dividends and with new and abiding satisfactions for all.

There is nothing here to be lost except by delay or self-deception. There is everything to gain—provided you make a plan, set dates for accomplishment, and get on with it. Your interim reports and the report to be made at the end of the postcampaign period can be professional performance at its shining best.

Section 3

Things to Know More About

Thoughts for Development Offices
Ten Special Aspects of Fund-Raising
Professional Help: When, Why, and How
Leadership Should Have Two Dimensions

Chapter 7

*Thoughts
for
Development
Offices*

$\mathcal{T}$he word "development," which Scott M. Cutlip says was first used in fund-raising by President Ernest DeWitt Burton of the University of Chicago in the autumn of 1924, should not be taken merely as another word for raising money, but as a broad term for the planned promotion of understanding, participation, and support. And it is in that light, I strongly suggest, that development offices should be planned, set up, and run.

The aims of this chapter are to explore for development offices of all kinds the fundamentals of purpose, policy, and program and to suggest some simple and useful ideas about structure, tools, and staff. But here at the beginning, there are two over-all thoughts that should be stressed and well understood.

First, I think, is that the development office has now become a full-time and vital activity for nearly all voluntary institutions—not just for colleges and universities but also for schools, hospitals, state and local units of health agencies, welfare agencies, museums, the performing arts, and especially, perhaps, all the major instrumentalities of organized religion. No longer is development either casual or occasional, as it usually was some forty years ago. Nor is it a minor and relatively ignoble function, to be seen and heard only when the need for its fruits becomes obvious, desperate, and demanding. It is now a thing of our time and a part of our future. And the broader its tasks and the higher its institutional level, the better job it will do.

Second is that these offices are for all sizes and scopes of institutions. Edgar M. Gemmell put this in a memorable way when he told the American Alumni Council at Miami on July 11, 1961, "The 76 trombone approach is clearly a possibility for only a limited number. It is well to remember that there have been occasions when masses have been swayed by a single piper." So whatever the suggestions may be in the brief pages that follow, let's all remember that substantial merit is never the child of multiples alone and that one good man, now as always, can make the light shine and work his wonders.

Purpose, Policy, and Program

Getting down to the specifics, the purpose of any development office at whatever kind of institution should be simply to develop support by service and gifts.[5]The direct role in the area of fund-raising itself is to promote all three legs of the fund-raising tripod—occasional capital campaigns, consistent annual giving by all elements of the constituency, and the promotion of deferred giving through bequests and living trusts. The indirect role in the area of public relations— because it is development's very lifeblood—is to sustain a critical awareness and a lively concern for the ways in which the institution deals with the arts and graces of appreciation, hospitality, responses to suggestions and criticisms, and all the other major processes of dealing with its constituency— past, present, and future. Whatever the size or nature of the cause or institution, purpose should never aim for less than this or attempt to do much more.

Policy questions are numerous and crucial. To begin with, the office must have quick and easy access to the administration, the trustees, organized units of the constituency, and all institutional bulletins and publications; not merely by administrative edict or unspoken consent but as a matter of serious and settled policy. Preferably, the director of development or his equivalent should attend trustee meetings and be present at all policy discussions—not for his vote, but for his information and grasp of background. The office should be aimiably receptive to suggestions and flexible on procedure, but openly and persistently adamant on long-term values as against the quickie stuff, and on the observance of all the tested fundamentals and sequences. Indeed, the tougher the stand the office takes on these matters, the faster it will earn approval and confidence.

The wise staff will never need to have imposed upon it the policy that its role is quiet and effective service rather than overt leadership, that its loyalty and adherence to the committee system is complete and unequivocal, and that its preference is always for strong and active lay leaders. William J. Trent, Jr., for many years the able executive director of the

United Negro College Fund, has punctuated this point by observing that over the years the fund learned "that generally the best leadership that you can find is among the people who are the busiest" and that the first-class attention of a second-class leader is often preferable to the second-class attention of a first-class leader—especially when the top citizen is tired, has stopped shooting for the moon, and has lost some of the gloss of his prestige and influence.

The good pros know better than anyone else how right Jethro was when he urged his son-in-law Moses to divide the work under the strongest captains he could find. Conversely, they know too that rapid deterioration will come to any development office that suffers weak leaders gladly or puts up very long with backing and advocacy that is anything less than first class, both in its influence and in the attention it gives the job.

Next, it should be both policy and practice to take the position that development is everybody's business and that the business is more good fun than hard work. Only fools and fatheads, in my experience, ever seek to build an image of the special cult, the mystique, and the ways of an inscrutable *expertise*. It gets nowhere to play an Atlas staggering around bravely under an intolerable load or a Job groaning over his many troubles. Optimism and universality should characterize the whole development operation, with confidence in all directions as the constant target.

I believe too that every development office, as a matter of settled policy, should take every available chance to play up the vital importance of the budget's private sector—regardless of the big and growing part played by governmental and other sources of institutional income. And it should never tire of preaching the gospel of thoughtful, proportionate, and dependable giving. For while the old words may get tiresome in the minds of the staff and the temptation to try something new may be hard to resist, the educational job that has to be done never changes, never gets any easier, and simply has to be repeated as the constituency fades out at the top and is refreshed from below.

Finally, in this selection of policy points, I would urge that no development office should ever willingly undertake any new activity or new project without a plan, a budget, and a staff. I've seen, as other veterans have, many a staff portfolio literally choked to death because additional function has been assigned without the necessary tools, man-hours, and money for expenses. The willing horse may win admiration, but he seldom wins races.

Whatever the policies, may I add, they should be spelled out clearly and shown around wherever it will do the most good. Everything, you will find, works better that way.

Variation is of course inevitable, in scope, magnitude, goals, and procedures. But whatever the variety, some fundamentals belong in every program.

The job begins, I think, with a clear and simple definition of what the institution wants to do, with approximate priorities, and how much it needs in terms of voluntary aid and financial support. With this there should be a list of opportunities for service and gifts, ranging from the modest and simple on up to the vital and heroic maximums. Both are constantly needed for all three legs of the fund-raising tripod—capital appeals, annual giving, and bequests—and should be kept up to date by representative review and fresh decision not less than once a year. Needful to say, the more substantial involvement that can be brought to bear on this process, the readier the acceptance and the prompter the advocacy.

A concurrent process is an objective and continuing analysis of the constituency—all the sources of voluntary aid and financial support. This is a task that must be complete and correct, as all list work should be, but it is worth emphasizing that the approach to the task should also be thoughtful and selective. Cover the ground thoroughly for all obvious adherents and possible converts, of course, but don't waste time or money trying to list and evaluate all the foundations, all the firms and corporations, and all the nonaffiliated people thought to be rich. But do give special attention to all past and present donors, and consider carefully what ought to be done to cultivate and enlist the aid of students and program staff. And whatever you do, don't overlook the widows. At all times the development office should be ready to nominate the top ten prospects for any big job or any big gift.

Knowing what has to be sold and knowing the market, next on the program comes the major task of volunteer enlistment, beginning with activation by involvement. This, like everything else, should proceed from the inside out, beginning with the trustees, the staff or the faculty, and the resident family in general. You have to have examples worthy of emulation, and you have to have available the advocacy and testimony of those who are there and thus know better than anyone else the institution and its program. The rest has to be done by field work and by on-the-site meetings, convocations, seminars, special dinners, and any other kind of planned event that has enticement and involvement value. The scenic wonders alone won't do it any more than the flora without honey will attract the bee. There must be bait at its best to arouse pride of association, to evoke concern for the continuity, and to stimulate confidence.

And as for field work, it is worth repeating that what I've always called "sea-gull visitation"—swooping in and swooping out—is almost always a waste of time and money. If there are not enough people to do the job thoroughly, or not enough time or travel money, then pick out fewer cities to visit, and visit them well, counting on hearsay and osmosis to spread the tidings to other places.

Adequate staff work, with reasonably frequent visitation, is all the more necessary for the well-established rule that local leadership is very much like an eight-day clock: without attention it will run down and stop in just about that time. And the staff alone can't keep things moving. The local leaders need the letters and phone calls from the president of the institution, the board chairman, and any others whose good opinion counts for something; not mere whip-cracking, but with messages aimed at hearts and egos. ("We're anxious for Cleveland to make a fast and impressive move so we can use it on Detroit. I'm going to report to the trustees at their meeting next week, and I know they'll be wanting to know what some of our top local leaders are doing and what their thoughts are.")

To ensure uniformity of inquiry and response and thoroughness in coverage, always employ questionnaires for the field worker's kit, particularly when someone unskilled in field work is doubling in brass by taking on the visit as an extra job. Finally, all field work should have a standard report system—for the information of other staff people, for committee members who may be concerned, and especially to enable higher-ups to write notes of appreciation to the key persons seen who were helpful to the field worker or agreed to perform one or more acts of service. Serendipity, it should be observed, regularly comes into play in field work well done. The aim may be in the area of fund-raising, but the rewards may accrue elsewhere.

A running record on cultivation procedures is an important element in development programs, and this necessitates a date file, to remind you whenever some person or situation is due for renewed attention. Cultivation itself, of course, deserves first-class attention, and every development program should have an approved list of all the possible procedures —advance mailings of special material, invitations to dine with the high brass, preferably black tie, requests to speak, to write pieces for the magazine, and to consult with career-seeking students, and anything else of the sort that soothes the spirit, calms the fears, and summons pride and concern. Just remember, whenever any thought at all is being given to cultivation, that everyone wants to be sought and wants to be a worthwhile member of a worthwhile group.

In this connection, there is hardly any procedure to compare with the all-around values of visiting committees. Given the right aura of prestige and lifeblood of sound and regular activity, a visiting committee is a thing beyond price. If you have them, nourish them well. If you don't have them, get them as soon as you can. And settle for nothing but the very best.

The development office may or may not have jurisdiction over the news bureau, the publicity department, the office of information, or any other institutional device for peddling the golden words. It has an obligation, nevertheless, to see that what is said or printed is consistent with development aims, that all the good rules of repetition are observed, that the timing of announcements leaves room for selective advance notices, and that speakers going out on the road are provided with the current data that will anticipate common questions and prepare them for the discussion periods that should follow all set speeches.

Similarly, while the processes of gift acknowledgment may be in the treasurer's domain, every development office should take a lively interest in how appreciation is expressed, how work subsequent to gifts is reported to the donors, and in general how the institution observes all the good rules about recognition and reward.

My final suggestion on program—with a reminder that these thoughts are for all varieties and sizes of voluntary agencies—is that development officers should find ways to visit regularly with their opposite numbers at comparable institutions. Attending the big conventions can be rewarding, provided you really work at it, but interinstitutional liaison by personal visits is important too. In no other way can you keep your views quite so fresh, your mind quite so open, or your perspective quite so clear. Never tell yourself, or let anyone else tell you, that you are too busy to do this.

Structure, Tools, and Staff

After purpose, policy, and program, people often ask what the basic structure of a development office should be.

The minimum requirements are simple enough. The office should first be anchored to the board of trustees, in that there should be a regular committee of the board to address itself to resources and development, to help set policy, to receive and make reports, and to front for the development office whenever it needs top help. Then, like every good home, the office needs a smart and dedicated woman—to police the housekeeping details, keep the records straight, watch the calendar, and keep things moving.[16] Somewhere too there has to be a good writer, and a good front man for outside contacts. Perhaps the director of development has both of these talents, or thinks he does. In any case, somehow, the president or the top brass ought to make sure that the office has the competent services of some smart woman, has the values of good writing, and a face that can be turned confidently toward the outside world. No office can get along even passably without these three things.

As for maximums, development offices these days run into staffs numbered by the dozen or more. The director can have associates not merely for all the major units in the institution and for all three legs of the fund-raising tripod, but also for all major divisions of the constituency, such as corporations, foundations, parents, and so on. Parkinson's laws acquire broad meanings here, but with due prudence there should be no real cause for alarm. No institution I have ever seen or heard of has enough staff to do what ought to be done. The only rule that seems to make good sense is to let growth come gradually, as the importance and urgency of function proves itself and becomes clear to all.

What tools are needed? The usual items, all of which serve the double purpose of keeping things straight and creating confidence, include an organization chart, the card system, a date file, an operating calendar to go up on the wall, and some variety of visual aids. Some use portable colored slides, and the more affluent often have motion pictures. But even a simple photograph album can serve the purpose, the point being that people always need help in visualization, and frequently are moved by it. As stated elsewhere, the minimum printed material should include an eloquent return envelope, bulletins or reports (the *Kiplinger Washington Letter* is a good model, both for style and layout), and a pocket-size piece summarizing the current and long-term goals—all of these with just enough copy to make the figures come alive and enough responsible names to beget confidence.

The choice of tools should be judged by what makes good conversation rather than merely a good impression. As law schools have found in teaching law and as all the good saints found in the days of the parables, cultivation and education by the case system have much to recommend them. A number of simple and brief case histories having to do with the philanthropic history of your institution—interesting stories of things done by interesting people—make for good conversation and provide good examples for others. This is especially true, I think, in bequest work, in approaches to relatives and widows, and in any kind of conversation where the opening gambit may be hard to find. Case histories of this sort may well justify a special leaflet, should be sprinkled here and there in bulletins and reports, and certainly should be at tongue's end for all development representatives, lay or professional. The aim here, and with all the chosen tools, is to seek grounds for dialogue rather than monologue and to lead always toward confidence, pride, and involvement in program. Anything else, however fancy or plausible, should be suspected as mere scenery.

And now, what kind of staff is needed for all these vital ventures?

Gemmell has pointed out, quite sensibly, that the resident wizards can't all be chiefs; some of them have to be just ordinary Indians. But high brass or low tin, aside from all the copybook maxims, the first thing to say, I think, is that all development people simply have to have the respect of program people and that the best way to earn such respect, in the words of John F. Kennedy, is "to do things well, and to do them with precision and modesty."

This is especially true in the field of education, where the understanding and respect of the faculty is a paramount necessity. For this, above all places probably, is where development people have to live with the eggheads, get along with the hardheads, and put up unceasing battle with the Harvard law of animal behavior: "Under carefully controlled conditions, organisms behave as they damn well please."

Great gobs of time and money have been spent in the veri-
fication of the fact that the young and hungry, especially
those with ears open and mouths shut, make better staff
workers than the elderly or the retired. Some experience is
no handicap if the ruts haven't closed the mind. And no
experience at all should be no bar to employment, provided
the prospective worker has dedication, habits of success,
eagerness to learn, and enough of what we Middle Westerners used to call "the old spizzerinctum." The complete
tyro, on the other hand, is usually a hazardous leap toward
some kind of disaster. He has the wrong convictions, the
wrong ideas, and all the wrong attitudes. One good specimen
of such a tyro was described a few years ago by one of the
senior old pros in these terms: "It isn't that he doesn't know
anything. What troubles me is that he doesn't even suspect
anything."

Good people for development work are hard to find. Sometimes they have been discovered in other parts of the same
vineyard or at comparable institutions at a different level—
people, for example, with dead-end jobs as teachers in secondary schools, who would welcome a development role at a college. Sometimes the institution pirates staff from fund-raising
firms, and sometimes good men indeed are found among the
younger volunteer workers. On the other hand, there are
dangers to avoid: the type of applicant who is merely tired of
what he has been doing, and wants to find a softer spot;
the Narcissus complex that leads a top administrator to seek
only those who seem to be in his own image; and the always
hazardous failure to read letters of recommendation for what
is not there. In fairness all around, both the person and the
spouse should be seen and dunked into the environment long
enough to bring out reliable impressions both ways.

"Hire 'em slowly, and fire 'em fast" is a good rule, remembering that careful and dependable mediocrity is much to be preferred to the kind of easy affability or occasional brilliance that too often is sustained either by the Martini crutch or by hopeless addiction to the needs of a starving ego.

Finally, as to staff, the good administrator sees them often, welcomes those who present problems along with ideas of their own, runs well-planned staff meetings, rejects the rough draft, defines clearly his requests for service, helps cheerfully when he has to help, gives earned credit and deserved praise, and feels free to cater always to the right kind of personal and professional pride. As they say in the Navy, he runs a tight ship but a happy one. (See other ideas about staff in Chapter 10.)

Easy Tasks and the Hard Ones

So now, what's hard and what's easy? Well, the relatively easy development projects are (1) those stimulated by conditional gifts, started by the two Rockefeller foundations more than fifty years ago and more lately exemplified in a truly big way by the Ford Foundation, (2) those in aid of youth, and (3) those plainly in the self-interest of the donor or in the defense and extension of values close to his heart. The classic toughies, on the other hand, are such things as buildings already up but not paid for, memorial projects already named but not fully financed, funds of any kind for which the easy money has been skimmed off at ruinously low standards for giving, and then of course such necessary but unexalted projects as new chimneys for power plants. Toughest of all, many old burns and scars will testify, is probably the "quiet special-gifts effort."

Chester E. Tucker, old friend and colleague, formerly vice-president for development and public relations at the University of Pennsylvania, and now a fellow consultant, gave us the right word about this in a notable paper, "Getting the Special Gift":

> Small gifts are important, even essential, because the big prospect is impressed by seeing a wide volume of support. . . . Thus it is that a so-called "quiet special gifts campaign," or what you might call a "still hunt" for large gifts, which sounds good in theory, is not really so good in practice. Both the solicitor whom you enlist to work, and the substantial prospect whose gift you are trying to get, want to know that many others are working in the interest of the cause and that many others are giving according to their means. Thus both the special gift and the average gift are important to you. More than that, there is no way to determine which of your small givers today will be your institution's major givers 20 years from now.

Values of Liveliness, Sensitivity, and Perspective

Generally, development people should cultivate three key attributes. First, there is a kind of liveliness that generates and communicates enthusiasm, knows and likes people by instinct and preference, exhibits a genuine kind of pleasure and gratitude for good advice and wise talk, and bears proudly the mantle of the job. Then there is sensitivity—to people, to ideas, to environments—without which, in some adequate degree, failure in this or any other field of personal service is almost certain. And the third value to be nurtured is perspective.

Perspective means lots of things to development offices, and all the things mean a lot. It means, for instance, that you never overlook the law of diminishing returns, that choices always have to be made between what is desirable and what is really necessary, and especially, perhaps, that the good laws and principles of organized fund-raising are a priceless gift of the long years, and can be ignored or trifled with at your peril. Perspective is important too in the area of personal advancement. For your role in this field is out in the wings, and not stage center. Your joys must be vicarious, and you must learn that they can be all the sweeter thereby. Let me repeat what you should remember in your own selfish interest—that to seek credit is to lose it and that to disclaim credit is usually to win more than you probably deserve.

Finally, I'd say go for stretch, play for confidence, and always leave a little room in your plans for help and advice. Avoid if you can the annual temptation to find novel ideas and fresh lines for copy; on the contrary, seek maximum mileage for the tested prose and the proved ways to get thoughtful and proportionate support. Don't be afraid to look a little puzzled once in a while, and never lose a good chance to say you don't know, but you'll try to find out.

"Development" is a dynamic word. It is a catalyst. And it always works best by dialogue and reciprocal action. So the closing words here have to be these: know your background, study your people, plan your course, and then, for Pete's sake, get out there and do your stuff.

Chapter **8**

Ten Special Aspects
of Fund-Raising

Special presentations   Bequest programs
National health agencies   National causes generally
Alumni funds   Church canvasses   Global appeals
United funds and community chests
Public relations and publicity   Memorial campaigns[17]

$\mathcal{M}$any special topics get involved in fund-raising. There are
the foundations, for example, and their close cousins the
modern corporations. These two in particular have been
covered sufficiently for my purposes in preceding chapters
and in the following section about special presentations. And
for those who want more detail, there are many books and
monographs about foundations and corporations, and many
better authorities.

My ten selections for this chapter, prompted both by
experience and by the suggestions of colleagues, are all wor-

thy of longer treatment—but far out of scale with the aims and scope of this book. So I propose merely to present some condensed notes—either what seems to be the essence of the topic or what has appeared to call clearly for a few special remarks. You won't find any definitive solutions here, but you ought to pick up useful suggestions and reminders.

Special Presentations

Miss Gertrude Moore, philanthropic secretary to Edward S. Harkness some forty years ago, was the first to tell me that institutional memoranda seeking gifts from such offices should cover in order the four topics of the problem, the proposal, the cost, and the opportunity. Arthur Packard, when holding the same post for John D. Rockefeller, Jr., used to say that special presentations should escape the trivial image by covering at least ten pages and should avoid the risk of tedium by not going much beyond fifteen. In all the intervening years, I have not heard better or more practical advice.

Almost every cause of any magnitude has to have a whole series of special presentations; for foundations, corporations, and individuals to be solicited for lofty or special projects. Such memoranda are almost always typed rather than printed, and double-spaced with adequate margins. They can have special covers, exhibits, and addenda, but should steer clear of obscure or pedantic terminology, the trick effect, the *avant-garde* layout, the overlong paragraph, and the ponderous type of prose. Serious indeed all the copy can be, but I would hope never solemn. Finally, if not delivered by hand, they should of course have a covering letter.

Introducing the problem, the presentation should explain its relationship with the total or general problem, the handicaps involved by things as they are, and perhaps expert and disinterested testimony on the points of importance and urgency.

Next, the proposal itself should embody the essence of the idea, how the project was developed, the reasons for proceeding in the way suggested, testimony on the soundness of the plan and the competence of the operating team to be in charge, and some degree of persuasive assurance that the plan has survival values and thus is apt to have a long, happy, and fruitful life.

The section on cost should show how the cost was estimated, what other funds if any are available, what net amount is now needed, how and when funds could be given to keep the project on schedule, and what action by this particular donor is now suggested.

Last, like all good concluding rhetoric, should come the sales pitch about the significant opportunity involved in this project—its possible value as a model leading to similar advances elsewhere, the ways in which this step forward would move other parts of the total program to higher levels, the possible implications for memorials, the impact of the gift on the institution's staff and constituency, and so on. The time factor can usually stand one more mention at this point, but the close should be an offer to consult or supply further data.

Putting it last for the extra emphasis, my final advice about special presentations is that they should be carefully planned and duly briefed.

Bequest Programs

In the tripod of development work (annual giving, occasional capital giving, and bequests) it is the bequest programs that generally have had the least consistent attention. Many important institutions have had no such programs at all.

The reasons are not hard to find. Some institutions are lucky enough or famous enough to get lots of bequests without looking for them in any organized way. Then there is almost always some initial reluctance to discuss bequest programs, if only because of the traditional attitude that man's ultimate fate never ranks high as a popular or tasteful topic for casual conversation. There may still be too much faith in the old method of merely putting out a booklet full of forms and eloquent quotations—and then waiting for lawyers and trust officers to get the appropriate action. Quite often, the constituency is allowed to believe that bequests and talk about bequests are only for the rich, the aged, and the infirm. The most important reason of all, within my experience, is a simple lack of the necessary dynamics, which are obtainable only by a plan, a workable program, effective leadership, consistent public exposure, and competent personnel.

The records throw valuable light on all this. There has been no measurable resistance, for example, to any man-to-man discussion of wills; on the contrary, as the YMCA has found in all parts of the country, there is always a cheerful reception when one trustee or committee member asks another, "Say, Bill, does your will provide something for the YMCA?" And another comforting finding has been that voluntary institutions are on sure and safe ground when they link their bequest programs to the doctrine that every man and woman should have a will and that wills should be kept up to date. About half the people, and even some 30 per cent of the lawyers, have no wills at all. And because Congress keeps changing the tax laws, wills can get out of date faster than women's hats, and perhaps for more palpable reasons. Banks, be it remembered, welcome trust business but don't write wills. Most lawyers who write wills do so more as a matter of client accommodation than as a source of profitable practice. And lawyers can't advertise. So voluntary institutions have a relatively clear field, as a service to their constituencies, for beating the tom-toms in favor of making wills and keeping them up to date.

There are at least two schools of thought about putting dynamics into bequest programs. The Western school is typified by Leland Stanford University, where since 1937 bequests and living trusts have been promoted with phenomenal success by staff activity alone—in what is most easily described as a rifleshot system of personal calls on those in a position of influence, rather than on persons considered as direct prospects. On the other hand, the Eastern school, typified by Yale and originating since World War II, aims for universality more than selectivity and operates almost entirely by a staff-directed committee system. These two methods are responsive to the traditions and habit patterns of their areas, and they both work well. And it should be added that they both prefer simple printed material and insist on sticking to the functions of promotion and letting the lawyers practice law.

The rules advocated here are for institutions of all kinds that operate by the committee system. What they need first of all, it has been found, is an image of universality. And there is no better way to accomplish this, so far as I know, than to urge the perpetuation of the interests of an active lifetime by capitalizing one's annual giving. This makes a floor everyone can stand on and has something in it for the giver as well as the institution.

Two fears usually arise when this approach is first suggested: either that it may lead to trivial bequests, when taken literally by those whose annual gifts are relatively nominal, or else that some really rich constituent may thus be led to make a bequest far below his potential. The answer to the fear of triviality is that while the publicity is general, the promotion is specific—and aimed always where it will do the most good. Only the promotion will get action. And the other answer is that the actual experience of the last ten years shows that bequests from the very rich average much higher than their capitalized annual giving—especially when it has been explained, as it always should be, that the capitalized-annual-giving story is meant to be a floor for all, and not a ceiling for those with a longer and higher reach.

Beyond this basic pitch for universality, the bequest program, by whatever method, should be ready from the very beginning to substantiate its reason for being. It can do so readily enough by citing historical precedents; John Harvard's tombstone is in Charlestown, for instance, but his monument is in Cambridge. It can also say some encouraging words about endowment, despite the smaller and smaller part played in today's budgets by endowment income. Certainly there can no longer be any fear of excessive endowment, as there was in the days of Chicago's great philanthropist, Julius Rosenwald. He disapproved of endowment funds on principle and liked to say, some forty years ago, that endowed cats catch no mice. Today, I think, we would answer, fairly enough, by pointing out that unendowed cats win no blue ribbons.

And then, to be more specific, the official list of the institution's current and future needs should be made to show, at varying dollar levels, attractive opportunities for major and memorial bequests. Every good voice and all appropriate media should champion the program. Not once a year, but all the time, there should be unadorned announcements of current bequests, big and little, in the institutional bulletins and magazines. The promotion of any one leg in the development program should always mention the other two legs—in this instance including the bequest program. Persistent visibility the program must have. Nowhere, in fact, is it more important to heed the words of André Gide, the French author: "Everything has been said already, but as no one listens, everything must be said again."

In this connection, I know of no rule as such about booklets and manuals. At Stanford, so I'm told by David S. Jacobson, the man in charge, "we have a loose-leaf manual that is prepared to make it easy for the lawyers to get the answers they need when they want them, a general booklet more for the use of the layman, which sets forth different ways of giving and has some—but not very much—tax emphasis; finally, there are the occasional pieces that come out, such as, for example, when the 1964 Revenue Act was enacted."

All printed material in this field, in my opinion, should be designed primarily as conversation pieces for members of bequest committees, with all the good reasons, precedents, and opportunities, and with enough names of influential committee members to build confidence. The art work should be simple and quickly appealing. The type should be big enough for older eyes to read easily. And I think the format, whatever the exact size, should fit within a standard #10 envelope, both because it should be easy for committee people to carry in their pockets and because you do have to allow for a sizable distribution by mail—always with covering letters, don't forget. The mailing list should include your own list of selected lawyers, trust officers, specialists in estate planning, tax experts, and others in related fields whose knowledge of your program and possible advocacy might be useful to you. Ask for questions, offer to send further data, eschew the solemnity, and keep it simple.

Coming back to the rules, perhaps the most important of all is that no one—staff or laity—should be permitted to advocate bequests until after he has made one himself. This principle is supposed to hold true in any sort of fund-raising, but in bequest work, where the procedural steps are obviously more numerous and complicated and where inertia is likely to play such a heavy hand, it is believed today to be an absolute essential. It breaks the ice—as with special-gifts work in capital campaigns for education when the president himself makes an obviously sacrificial contribution. It makes for confidence in the program and confidence in the staff. And it tends to put just a little more gleam in the eye of the worker. He who advocates must first bequeath.

Almost as important is the rule that bequest programs should stick to established lines of organization and work from the inside out. Within each regular or officially organized group—preferably beginning with the administrative staff and the board of trustees—you get a chairman and get him to make his bequest. You then have the chairman recruit his committee and get them to make their bequests, and so on down through all the prospects in the top 10 per cent of your list, and eventually on out to the rest of your constituency. There is nothing more complicated about the process than making a snowman by first making a snowball.

There is only one admonition to be made here. Universality is the right stuff to talk about, and the orderly process is ever to be admired. But keep an eye on the actuarial tables. By which I mean, as I have said some years ago, that if there is a choice between explaining the program to a young man of seventy-five and a youth of sixty, do the more senior of the two the courtesy of the first talk.

Every bequest program certainly needs staff attention, but how much and of what kind is for every institution to decide for itself. David Jacobson and all four of his associates at Stanford are lawyers. I know of no Eastern institution that has more than one person doing the staff work, and most of those I know about serve on part time and carry other duties.

Legal training aside, the staff should have talents for promotion, rather than legal precision, and should know just enough about the law as it applies to bequest work to get around comfortably and affably and keep things going. The staff should know the institutional policy, should know how bequests are handled and the funds invested, and should be able to recite the good case histories applicable to varying situations. They should know how the different state laws affect bequests, especially when there are close relatives surviving, and what state laws have to say about the timing of charitable bequests. Most of all, however, they should know about people and how to get along with them, and should be moved by genuine dedication.

In summary, I would say that every bequest program needs what all other fund-raising programs must have, in terms of good planning, effective leadership, committed advocacy, adequate meetings, time schedules, good staff, enough expense money in the budget, and all the rest of it. But especially, because the road is long and the hurdles are many, does it need the impetus of words that have lasting powers to lift the vision, warm the heart, and move good spirits to responsible action.

My friends at New Haven, in discussing memorials man can erect "in places he has known and loved, which he believes will endure," described their program this way: "An opportunity for alumni and friends of Yale to give some cherished name, in the words of Pericles, 'a home in the minds of men.'"

The most potent prodder of all, however, since the laments of Ecclesiastes and long before, is the dictum, "You can't take it with you."

National Health Agencies

More than thirty agencies are in this field, raising annually about a quarter of a billion dollars—with more than 90 per cent of the money going as usual to the top ten, now headed by the American Cancer Society.[18]All of them, big and little, have special problems which are not generally understood and should be mentioned here.

Most of them have three functions—public education and research, which have to be directed and controlled nationally, and some sort of service to patients and their families, which has to be done locally, if at all. Both for effective program and for fund-raising, they need substantial power and visibility on the national level and, locally, adequate membership and influential representation. Few indeed have all this.

Here lies their common dilemma in raising money. They must try either to raise their own funds or to gain inclusion in locally federated appeals by united funds or community chests.

Raising their own funds nationally, it has been found by the hard road of trial and error, has become just about impossible. The big foundations are no longer interested in these annual and supposedly popular causes. The great corporations have learned to give almost exclusively through local influence. Benefit programs and telethons can get publicity but not much net return. And giant mail appeals, except for the sale of Christmas and Easter seals, have just about become a thing of the past.

Turning to federation, necessitating as it must some concession of self-interest in budget decisions, can bring and has brought a welcome degree of financial security but rarely any rapid growth in program. Even to gain admittance to these federated appeals, let alone to run a respectable second to the solely local agencies, requires influential representation and plausible proof of local performance in program.

The result has been that the strong national health agencies, with urgent convictions of growth potential going well beyond funds likely to be raised through federation, and convinced too that their message is too important to be buried among the stories of hundreds of other participating causes, have tended to go it alone. Weaker agencies, for the most part, have had to go it alone for the opposite reason: lack of power and influence.

This is why health agencies have to run collections rather than real campaigns and must depend so largely on mass response—with all that means in terms of personal significance to the individual, dramatization by symbols, slogans, and poster pictures of afflicted little children, proof of local or regional service, and all the techniques of recognizing and rewarding volunteer service.

Health-agency appeals do best when they stress the universal danger but at the same time show proof that progress is being made and that hope is getting brighter. For in this way they observe an ancient rule of human persuasion, by giving the people something to fear and something to look forward to. It follows that they have a strong case for adequate and far-flung research, despite the bigger funds now being appropriated for research by the Federal government. For here they can invoke a law or principle that has held true throughout human history in religion, politics, education, and all forms of human inquiry: namely, that creative minds seem to have a natural affinity for remote or obscure origins. So if you want to find such minds and help them on their way to triumph and immortality, you have to do as Peter did—fashion

a big net and fling it far and wide. This takes national decision and a great deal of money. And of course they have a
good story too about the need for public education, if only
on the prompt recognition of symptoms and the fundamentals of proper medical care.

The common hurdles of these health agencies are over-
reliance on publicity, subscription envelopes, and other
printed material that tends to promote low standards of giving, and failure to do enough selective solicitation for gifts of
$25 or more. Some of them have problems too in the general
practice of percentage financing, by which local chapters or
committees retain a certain percentage of the net funds
raised and send the balance to national headquarters. When
this deal is 50-50, or say 60-40, the result still flouts the rules
of good budgeting but works fairly well. But when the division is 90-10, national activity suffers from malnutrition, and
the favored communities that can raise the most money tend
to build up unused surpluses, while the communities with
most of the health problems but the least potential for raising money tend toward local programs much more meager
than they should be—with national headquarters unable to
help them.

National activity, well done, is a fine thing indeed.
Regional or state activity is the best possible level for educational meetings and staff seminars. But when it comes to
raising money, there is still no substitute for leadership that
leads, rather than big names that merely shine, and nothing
that works quite so well as the simple printed piece that opens
the way to good conversation. No health agency, in fact, ever
has anything better than the dedicated and informed volunteer who brings the cause to its court of final appeal—just by
coming up on your porch with good materials in his hand and
ringing your doorbell.

National Causes Generally

Much of what has been said about the health agencies applies equally to national causes in general—the family service agencies, the USO, the YMCA, the YWCA, the YMHA, the CYO, scouting, and so on. The big difference is that these agencies, except those in the fields of religion and foreign relief, are usually financed by federation. Some of them with percentage financing, like the YMCA, can budget their programs only after the money has been raised. Others, like the USO, must have advance programs with price tags in order to make fund-raising proposals and then need operating programs later on, depending on how much money was raised, how much was collected, and how much has been made available for them. Like the health agencies too, their competition with local interest—even within their own organizations—is constant and severe. Any time the national interest appears to threaten local budgets or programs, the battle flags are sure to fly.

Long and tough experience in this field has brought out clearly a few conclusions that should interest anyone carrying the fund-raising responsibility for a national cause.

In the beginning, while there is still a chance to see to it, the national cause should be given a name that works at all levels. The National War Fund of World War II found itself at a disadvantage in getting common identification at state and local levels because of the word "national." "United" would have been a better key word: "United War Fund of Ohio" and "United War Fund of Lima." That way, the general program of publicity and advertising could mean the same thing everywhere.

Policy should restrict national functions to matters which

can be dealt with in no other way; all else should be delegated to regional, state, or local bodies. And this should work both ways. National headquarters should mind its own business, and will get faster and more complete acceptance if it does. But it is also important that national headquarters should flatly refuse to attend to anything that could or should be handled locally. Limit your functions, and then perform them boldly—there is a good rule indeed. It avoids the weakening compromise and lets you fight like a wildcat for what is really yours.

Strong management and direction is doubly difficult for these national agencies. The first reason is that boards tend to weaken when nominations are made either for the name-glitter of so-called "personalities" or as rewards for local service, rather than for the injection of fresh power and influence at a level where respect is more to be admired than authority. And the other reason is that national executives are so often really chosen by, and beholden to, the executives in the big cities that they tend to be of service instead of tending to lead. This situation is aggravated much of the time by percentage financing, in which the big cities have the controlling power. The results here, even though the national executive were to have all the virtues of Moses, Jeremiah, and Paul, are apt to be more homily than hell-raising. (And of course this is something more to be indulgently understood than quickly solved.)

National bodies should solicit money nationally only to help set standards of giving, to launch projects outside the regular budget, or when the properly delegated solicitation has been balked or proved fruitless. Even for these special purposes, no great results should ever be expected. Approval should never be given for the delegation of fund-raising to fraternal bodies, patriotic societies, or luncheon clubs—for the practical reason that unit gifts from organizations like this are always at a substantial discount, because all the individual members can give so nominally. And I suppose it should be added, for readers who may have come in late, that national agencies should have tough and clear policies on raising money by benefits, telethons, raffles, or any other devices which look like easy short cuts but which even at their best have the deplorable effect of weakening or destroying local responsibility for organized fund-raising.

Whenever possible, printed materials should leave space for local imprints. Special attention must be paid to the big cities because they have most of the money. Field workers should be top people or else stay home. The representation of race, creed, and color has to be recognized all the time and all the way, both in appointments and function. And finally, after many pleasant years in these vineyards, I'd like to say that once in a while you have to leave the safe and sure ground, as little Eliza did, when you really want to get somewhere and get there quickly.

Alumni Funds

Our oldest alumni fund is at Yale, where in 1890 they agreed on these principles: that the funds should be unrestricted; that the appeal should be universal; that emphasis on numbers would actually encourage larger special gifts; and that the primary objective should be to persuade the alumni to give annually, with such a steady flow of contributions that the alumni themselves might properly be regarded as an endowment, with the fund's yearly receipts as the income. So what's new?

Today's procedures, seventy-five years later, are based on all those original ideas. The differences can be summarized by the general observation that there is no longer anything casual or merely traditional about the way alumni funds raise money. They still like to aim high for the percentage of the constituency that responds, but their main target is now a dependable flow of such thoughtful and proportionate giving that the amount of dollars will keep steadily climbing with each successive year and always approaching the maximum that can then be raised. Their new importance has been emphasized at a number of institutions as coming first in the scheme of things for raising money. They have the honor, the recognition, and the precedence.

This new look, of course, takes superior leadership, a good case, and competent staff work. It has meant putting fresh emphasis on negotiated class quotas, some equivalent of special handling for the top 10 per cent of every list, cross solicitation by regional or local committees, and, in many cases but not always, backing up individual class agents by the appointment of representative class committees, thus bringing in the influence of the high school ascots as well as the prestige of the old school tie. It has meant more staff, more field work, more meetings, more budget, and stronger effort all around.

Condensed as the notes in this chapter are supposed to be, I think everyone interested in fund-raising—whatever the field —can learn something useful and improve his general understanding by reviewing some of the lessons learned by alumni funds since World War II.

Principally, my notion is, they have learned what community chests and capital campaigns learned many years ago: to apply some of the best techniques of special-gifts work. The 174 top prospects in the class of 1923 at Harvard were all seen personally, with the result that the fortieth-reunion gift of that class, with a goal of $200,000, finally reached $242,084.03. The top half of Princeton's list gives 93 per cent of the money, and about half the money comes from the 4 per cent of the list that gives $200 or more. At Yale, the all-time champion, 15 per cent of the donors in reunion classes give 85 per cent of the money, and 15 per cent of all donors give about 80 per cent of the money.

As one might suppose, all such efforts stress the advantages of giving securities and on their subscription blanks always mention securities as well as checks. And how this pays off, in a gradual but progressive way, is illustrated by the growth figures given me by Yale's Charles Watson, III. It is worth noting, I think, that in Charlie's sixteen years in charge of the alumni fund he has demonstrated over and over again that the arts of promotion work better when you have a good nose for the kind of statistics that can illuminate your plans. Like these:

Year	Total raised	Donated securities	Per cent of total
1951	$1,010,324	$ 63,000	6.2
1955	$1,302,324	$225,000	17.2
1960	$2,313,131	$460,000	19.8
1965	$3,301,943	$910,532	20.7

Other funds have moved toward higher standards of giving by organizing "century" clubs, aimed at moving small gifts up to $100 or more, and clubs with other names aimed at moving more donors up to the level of $1,000 or more. These devices have worked well wherever the advantages of moving up the small donors have outweighed the risk of moving some big donors down.

"Matching gift" programs in corporations, in which certain companies will match the giving of alumni on their payrolls, have added materially to the totals of some funds, and are widely regarded as a great thing for cultivating corporate and business interest. But so far the feeling is that they have been no more effective than the total effectiveness of the funds themselves.

Alumni who are involved in worthwhile groups of one kind or another or who as undergraduates did well in extracurricular activity work better and give more dependably than all others.

Class-agent lists need to be pruned regularly, or else the term of service should have a limit of perhaps five years. And while those who write their own appeal letters may be very good at it, all agents, I think, should be subject to some simple rules and criteria that are basic to raising money by mail.

Except where the manpower is too limited, alumni funds can be kept going throughout the time of capital campaigns, instead of being virtually shut down at such times, as they used to be. And they are now more apt to gain thereby than to lose. As a recent example, Amherst increased its annual giving from $335,000 to $409,000 during the time of its campaign for capital purposes. And this was no exception.

Basic changes, it should be noted, have never happened all at once. The surest way to bring about good change is never by fiat from headquarters, but by demonstration and osmosis. Let the way be shown by one or two classes or one or two communities, and others will be much more likely to follow.

Implied reproach, or suggestion of debt on the ground that the pay for education has never met its cost, has been universally poisonous, with alumni and more especially with parents.

Comparisons between funds are usually meaningless. There are far too many differences in what dollars get counted and which sources are included. And that goes for cost comparisons too.

Looking ahead and taking into account that annual giving seldom if ever takes any great leap forward, where are the potentials for doing better?

Parents would probably improve their giving if they too had more special-gift treatment, or at least a more selective choice of copy in the letters used. Alumni of graduate and professional schools might do better, as they have at Harvard and elsewhere, with more selective solicitation and a clearer definition of where self-interest fits their giving. Much more can be done, I think, in the solicitation of firms and corporations for unrestricted giving on an annual basis, probably with annual renewals for such commitments. Certainly we should bear in mind that corporate giving to education, wonderful as its brief record has been, is still in its legal infancy. Nobody really knows how far it can be expected to go.

Faculties, traditionally, have been protected from alumni funds, except as individuals happen to be graduates of the particular institution. With their pay now at much higher levels, with outside fees not unknown, and with their own self-interest so plainly involved, there is much to be said today for soliciting those members of the faculty who are not A.B. alumni of the institutions they serve, and especially those who have tenure. By all the rules about people, they too are people, and probably some 10 per cent of them have plenty of money.

Any college without a strong reunion-gift program, calling for the big push every five years, may escape the annoyances of "the postreunion slump," but is probably missing hundreds of thousands of dollars. Any job done about the same way year after year tends to slip into routine, whereas the best men available can be called upon for the occasional special effort. That, in fact, is why the occasional capital campaign usually gets the top leadership.

Most dependable of all, however, is digging out the sleepers —those Rip van Winkle contributors who have the potential for big giving but who have innocently, it should be assumed, acquired the habit of giving some small and fixed amount determined many years before. There are many such people on every list I have ever seen or heard about, and they are the hills where the best gold lies.

We should say too, if only to cover all the important ground, that there will always be work to be done and higher levels to seek, so long as every big institution, roughly, has about ten thousand alumni who give less than $10 a year. But don't hold your breath until that problem gets solved. Instead, my counsel is to stick to what works well, and don't let go.

Finally, the current significance of alumni funds is of vital general importance, for the good and obvious reason that education is now the key to our whole future. The gifts to these annual funds have been described as "the critical top 10 per cent of our budget," as "the margin for greatness," and as "the vital sector" of institutional income. Whatever percentage of the budget they may be, they are essential criteria for foundation and corporate support, which have a truly celestial preference to help those who help themselves. And because unrestricted money has no strings, it is both a compliment of confidence in the trustees and the administration and the best possible insurance for at least three vital freedoms—to choose those who teach, those who come to learn, and whatever a free faculty may decide should be explored and should be taught.

It is not too much to say, I think, that by the effect of their free dollars, and especially by their effect on key people, alumni funds are exerting enormous leverage on philanthropy in general and on the whole future of civilization. They deserve wide understanding and the best attention that can be made available.

Church Canvasses

Just as a footnote, because the general problem of church financing is far too big for inclusion here, I feel impelled to point out that the basic weakness of the standard "every-member canvass" is that not enough pains are taken to keep program out in front of fund-raising. For that purpose, indeed, the very phrase is wrong.

Exhortation in the pulpit does nothing for those not there. Mailed material alone achieves no involvement. Threatened failure is too often featured more than tales of success. At canvass time, the annual accent is on budget first and program second, with more of the visibility on the mechanics of raising money than on the joys of group action in common cause.

The annual process need not be such a worrisome thing, if only more pains were taken—long before canvass time—to remember what people tend to do and to get more of them involved in acts of service, which alone can create the sense of added responsibility that comes only through participation in program.

Even the mechanics are not handled too well; how often do you see in any every-member canvass a gift table showing the numbers and amounts of gifts needed in order to make the goal? Talk of tithing can indeed suggest higher standards of giving, whereas talk of averages can ruin them. But the only sure way to move the more remote members of the congregation to higher levels of support is to go out where they are and by influential advocacy get them involved in program. You have to pay attention, and you have to take pains.

Global Appeals

With two-thirds of the world's people always hungry and with a growing realization that voluntary acts of kindness do more for global friendships than parades of awesome power, it is no wonder that foreign relief appeals have grown both in volume and breadth of program, and will doubtless continue to grow—far beyond anything the past has ever seen.

Programs for feeding the hungry, mostly the children, are now a happy union of government action in supplying free foodstuffs and paying most of the huge costs of transportation, and voluntary action programmed and administered by some fourteen agencies, headed by the biggest of all, Catholic Relief Services, of the National Catholic Welfare Conference. In its latest year, this one agency helped some forty million needy persons without regard to race, creed, or color, distributed relief supplies in seventy-three countries, and collected and passed around overseas some 18 million pounds of good used clothing donated and made ready in parish houses all over the United States. Since its founding in 1943, this one agency has helped 420,544 refugees to find new homes in more hospitable lands.

With such massive service and with comparable programs conducted by the other agencies, both secular and religious, the response of the American people and their leaders to global appeals today probably gets the biggest value per dollar that our dollar has ever seen, in all three areas of health, education, and welfare.

Help for indigenous agencies overseas that are linked by world ties to national agencies here at home, such as the YMCA and YWCA, is also a growing development in American philanthropy, and seems to me to be far better understood than it was before World War II. It is probably all too true that we cannot export our political system. But we are succeeding very well indeed in exporting our committee system, with its attitudes and methods of organized self-help. This, in many lands, has brought improvement, hope, and genuine gratitude.

It has been my happy lot to have been involved in the financing of a number of these global programs. And my concern here is to summarize, with the help of good colleagues, some of the lessons of the past two decades.

First and foremost, I would urge all global causes to stick to their own established pipelines, never seeking wholly new or independent forms of organization, but rather fanning out by diocese or by already-established state or regional setups, and then—with consistent official help and sanction—moving to the parish, congregation, local association, or whatever the local unit may be. Even with all this ready-made system, the job is hard enough. Without the system, it would be better for all to let the project die at birth. And I think it is worth adding that even with all the established pipelines, no agency today should undertake a clothing collection for overseas without long and careful study. The amount of *expertise* involved and the red tape of permits, ocean freight, customs, and literally God knows what all are staggering in volume and complexity, and to me, after watching them for twenty years, almost incomprehensible.

Another lesson, ever persistent and troublesome, is that the staff management out in the regional or diocesan headquarters never seems to suffer gladly the routine of the annual seminars. Those who have done the job before, and perhaps many times, tend to feel that for them such meetings are superfluous. They know the story, they say, and they know what to do. But the meetings have to be held just the same, and always do a lot of good, providing fresh material for conversations back home, bringing a renewed sense of communion by personal association with others who have the same tasks to perform, and providing, even for those who doze, a little recharging of the batteries. These causes, like all major efforts, need an atmosphere of relevance, importance, and urgency. And for that nothing casual will ever do.

Next in importance, perhaps partly due to old doubts about "missionary work" and our understandable inability to grasp the meanings of giant problems far away, is the lesson that global appeals need the specifics of good case histories—pictures and stories of actual accomplishments in particular places. The story of mass unemployment, for instance, in and of itself has little impact; the concept is too general, and we have so much of it right here at home. You may have noted from news accounts alone, for example, that the response recently to the plight of just one small town in the mountains of Kentucky was much faster and aroused more action than the story of the general problems of Appalachia. Similarly, the good results for overseas appeals come when you talk about a trade school in the desert of Jordan for homeless boys or a farm program getting fabulous results in south India or Mexico. It is the story that stops them, just as it did in the days of the parables and as it does now, for instance, with the appeal of the *New York Times* Neediest Cases, which in 1964 set a new record of $709,886 from 15,202 contributions. As always, the story of the little Dutch boy gets more play than all the dikes in Holland.

As a natural corollary, the best basic appeal, and well suited to our American temperament and tradition, is to help others help themselves. This has been a mighty factor here at home in the success of the United Negro College Fund, which in some twenty brief years has raised approximately $80 million. And in the YMCA, my old friend Emery M. Nelson, who directed the successful Buildings for Brotherhood campaign before he went to George Williams College as vice-president for development, has this to say about that vital point:

> I think the easiest money we raised came after we had prepared the associations overseas to indicate what they would do, and to attain stretch goals in their own campaigns, with North American money as a conditional gift to be won by their own success. This was a powerful stimulant to the towns and cities overseas, and appealed strongly to those here at home with an old and deep-seated feeling that our brothers overseas accept funds but give little or nothing of their own. Americans will always show their concern to help people help themselves.

As Emery Nelson and others have also testified, it pays big dividends in global programs to be constructively grateful by reporting back on what was done with the contributed money. It pays too to urge fellow Americans, on trips abroad, to visit projects either on or close to their itineraries. For especially when project directors are advised of their coming and they make the visit and then come home, theirs is the best possible kind of eloquent advocacy—they were just there, and they saw the good work with their own eyes.

Corporations with business overseas, foundations and universities with regional experts, government agents and the officers and men of the armed forces, and often the resident members of American colonies abroad can all be helpful. Ask them to do something for your overseas cause. That way you get help, and you make more friends.

Finally, may I say again that general appeals by mail and other forms of publicity never go far on the road to Jericho. The surest and most productive way to raise money for global programs is to follow established channels, such as those of the church or the association. For that, like nothing else, takes you where the people are, for the telling of the story and for face-to-face talk.

United Funds and Community Chests

Here, surely, is the good meat and potatoes of all American fund-raising: financing by "the United Way" the growing and complex needs of recreation agencies, family and child care, health services, and in most places too the work of the American Red Cross. But so vast and steady has been the achievement that we've grown accustomed to its face, "like breathing in and breathing out."

There is no intention here to explain how federation works

its annual wonders or to presume to offer any operating ideas or suggestions. What I hope to do first is to give those engaged in fund-raising's other fields a little more background. And then, mainly for incoming staff people and newcomers to the lay leadership, I hope to provide some useful and significant perspective on federation's common aims and ideals, the chief lessons of the past twenty-five years, what the general troubles and threats now seem to be, and what any national agency should know about the processes of inclusion. Finally, I'd like to express a thought or two about the trends and opportunities of federation as they now look to me after eight or ten years of wartime and postwar experiences of my own and after another fifteen years of simply sitting up there with the cheering section.

The common aim of federated financing is easy to explain but hard to live up to: "to muster the maximum resources of any given community in support of well-planned, well-balanced and forward-looking programs by voluntary agencies—in such a way that everybody benefits when nearly everybody gives." Ideally, such an aim requires five indispensable ingredients: representative trusteeship, serving with equal fidelity the threefold interests of agencies, contributors, and the general public, freedom from partiality and compulsion, the sacrifice of self-interest so essential to all forms of effective cooperation, and the confidence and good will of all concerned. It follows, I think it is obvious, that federation too must put program ahead of fund-raising and can thrive only when its goals have relevance, importance, and urgency and when its atmosphere is consistently one of optimism and universality.

And then I suppose we should take a quick glance at the other side of this valuable coin: namely, that federation tends to get into trouble when preferential positions are allowed for one or more agencies, when inclusion procedures tend to be more compulsory than voluntary, or when trusteeship gets heavily weighted in the interest of special contributors. Happily, such error appears rarely; even a fine ointment like the balm of Gilead, let us remember, must have suffered an occasional fly.

So now let's look at the awesome record of these past twenty-five years.

In 1940, the year before Pearl Harbor, there were 561 chest campaigns, which raised for 1941 a total of $86,297,069—95.3 per cent of goal and 103.6 per cent of the total raised in the previous year. In 1964, after a quarter of a century more to be dimly remembered than consciously recalled, there were about 2,200 such campaigns—four times as many—and for the budgets of 1965 they raised $580,000,000, or 100.3 per cent of goal and 106 per cent of the previous year. So what was raised after this one generation of federation history was almost seven times as much as in 1940. By any index, this record is a great one indeed.

But of even more interest to any student of fund-raising is the persistent proof of these years that federation has been both bold and prudent. Only in the three fabulous years of World War II and again in 1964 were the total goals actually exceeded. And only in the two drop-away years right after that war did the totals fail to exceed the amounts raised in the previous years. Except for that span of extremes, 1943 to 1947, inclusive, federation always put stretch in its goals and showed steady improvement in total amounts finally raised. Boldness and prudence became a fixed and general tradition, and when the challenges of the war years opened up new horizons for the fund-raising potential, "the United Way" became possible for all and in 1949, in Detroit's first all-inclusive Torch Drive, became a shining and epoch-making reality.

Techniques for improving standards of giving, such as the

"Fair Share" plan, were constantly improved. Organized labor, as it had in the time of the National War Fund, began to exert a mighty influence—was one of the big factors in launching united funds in the larger cities, and is considered to have been significantly instrumental in raising the level of employee and executive gifts from 30 per cent of the total in 1955 to 56 per cent of the total in 1964. Semantics too took a hand during the period beginning after World War II, with "Once for All" honorably retired in favor of "the United Way." But all the way through, federation never forgot its own fundamentals, or got led astray from its main business. Most important of all, I'm sure many would think, it never forgot that its bread and butter is budgeting and balance.

Today's general troubles and threats are partly chronic and partly acute. Always, for example, we have with us those Cassandra-like voices, overimpressed by storied Kansas City, which keep warning us with solemn certainty that "they've gone about as far as they can go." There are always those too who would have the benefits of federation without its disciplines and who would bypass the function of budgeting by trying to promote agency designation through in-plant or other forms of partial federation—which in itself has ever been a source of disillusionment and discontent. Never, of course, are there enough competent and dependable people to go around —among the laity or for the staff. And then there is the chronic trouble that comes with age and time: the tendency, as in all human affairs, toward the deterioration that comes when incandescent eyeballs lose their luster and pride yields to complacency or fear.

Acute problems can be found where federation exists in name only, mostly for lack of top leadership and staff. Agency rebellion should be the cure, but sometimes gets stymied when many of the same people are involved in both agency and chest. Time should tell, but may not talk loudly enough for quite a while. The larger problems, however, are really worth true study, as they have their roots both in old fears of multiplicity in the health and welfare field and in the wholly new explosion of local campaign efforts for education and culture.

More of that a little later. Right here, however, may I insert a few bits of advice for national causes which may aspire to inclusion in federated campaigns.

First, it should be said that inclusion on favorable terms seldom comes about by mail appeals from elsewhere or brief personal visits by field representatives. Next, while it is true that a good chest or united fund may initially make a grant to a new outside agency based on what it raised by itself the year before, budgeting must eventually come back into the picture —in full competition with all the other member agencies. Another point to remember is that precampaign allotments are and must be purely provisional; what counts will be the post-campaign decisions, based on what was raised, and is likely to be collected. Most important of all, the outside agency must take into account the established fact that its proposed budget can never be fully financed by federation alone. For one thing, national cushions in quota systems rarely find ready acceptance. And when that is the case, the only ways the full budget could be financed would be that every chest would raise and collect its full goal, that the allotment to the outside agency would survive postcampaign budgeting in all communities, or that some especially virtuous few would grant more to make up for the shortages elsewhere. Such circumstances are not merely utopian; they are simply not to be found. So what are the outside national causes to do about all this? They can seek to understand federation's own problems. They can look before they leap, and then after they go in they can participate actively in the united job to be done. They can put on a dramatic and persuasive show at budget time, and they can be ever prepared to work hard and occasionally to yield on the troublesome points of autonomy, visibility, and self-interest. Just fussing up a breeze, as they say in North Carolina, will get them nowhere.

Coming back now to trends and opportunities, I first wish to quote my old friend and colleague Lyman S. Ford, one of the late and great Charlie Stillman's boys in his golden days at Ohio State—always a top workman and planner in the federation vineyard and since 1960 the executive director of federation's national body, United Community Funds and Councils of America:

> Through the years united campaign results have shown a close correlation with "disposable personal income." If this trend continues, it is possible that federated campaigns will be raising as much as $810 million by 1970. . . . Increasingly, federations are recognizing that their fund-raising operations not only must be effective in raising money but must be a positive influence in improving the quality and adequacy of all services, governmental and voluntary, and must aid in increasing public interest in, and understanding of, health and welfare needs and services. . . . Furthermore, united fund-raising makes its appeal to community leaders on the basis of their interest in the total community health and welfare, and develops citizens with this over-all point of view.

To this I would add, from my own experience and observation, that some of the current problems of federation may well turn out to be opportunities for broader service. And this has to do particularly with the competition for local support by firms and corporations on the part of two almost wholly new forces that have arisen since World War II: the appeals for higher education, with corporate giving newly legalized, and for such cultural causes as the performing arts, museums, libraries, ballet and theater groups, and other similar projects catering to leisure-time activities and sheer entertainment. Federation can hardly hope to encompass all of this, as it has with health and welfare. But it can help and assert leadership.

Older colleagues may remember Chester I. Barnard, former president of the New Jersey Bell Telephone Co. and wartime leader of the USO. One of his memorable sayings, I always thought, was to the effect that authoritative advice is to be preferred to authoritarian control. So in that light, why should not the good forces of federation hold the line on the scope of their own fund-raising, in all boldness and prudence, and at the same time extend the area of their interests and activities? I see the day coming, and hopefully near at hand, when lay and staff leaders of "the United Way" shall offer their wisdom and help to schools, colleges, universities, technical institutes, symphony orchestras, zoos and museums, resident opera and theatrical companies—and yes, perhaps even to the burgeoning appeals of organized religion. In ways like this, federation can still pursue its old and admirable aspirations toward better living for all—and much of the time in confident partnership with government, as urged recently by John D. Rockefeller, 3rd.

Mr. Rockefeller, in a memorable address at the 1964 inaugural dinner of the Federation of Jewish Philanthropies of New York, took the position that "philanthropy generally is not attuned to the tempo of the times."

Great as the role of government has become in the health and welfare field, as "part of the social history of our century," he said that comparable roles have now become essential in other fields too. "Some of the new needs that challenge our generation," he declared, "are so great, so important, so ramified, and often so immediate, that only government, working in dynamic partnership with private initiative, can attack them on the scale required." As an example, he pointed to the worldwide effort needed to stabilize population growth, where private groups can contribute much in the way of research and specialized knowledge but where the long-range responsibility "must rest squarely on government."

In other areas, he said, private citizens must carry the responsibility of leadership, with government playing a vital supporting role. He mentioned the field of the arts as an example, and cited New York City as having "long been a substantial factor in the financing of our museums and libraries."

"As government becomes a more active partner in our work," he said, "our private efforts assume even greater importance. . . . My faith in the American system makes me confident that we shall be equal to the task; that reasonable men working together will develop a relationship that will preserve and enhance private leadership."

Food is here, I submit, for further exploration by community chests and united funds of the ways in which government and private citizens can become better and confident partners in the advancement of new frontiers.

Thomas Mann once pointed out, "There is an element in American civilization which if universalized would bring about world peace." To me it seems fair to say too that there is an element in the principle of federation that merits stretching away up high, with the very best men each community can get and with the interest vested, not in "the United Way" itself or any other form of methodology, but in the community as a whole. The people will respond and follow, all the lessons tell us, when the image held before them is one of courage and confidence.

Public Relations and Publicity

These words get bandied about in all stages of fund-raising, and all too often as though they meant one and the same thing. Merely for the advancement of understanding, it seems worthwhile to make the basic distinction. It needs to be repeated that *public relations is a state of affairs—not a function in and of itself, and not to be confused with publicity.* (And where I come to speak of publicity, I shall add a few thoughts to those already expressed in Chapter 4, pages 42 to 44.)

Public relations activities, or programs, operate by the ancient law that actions speak louder than words. They are based on planned action, usually—and preferably action designed not merely to create publicity as such, but to affect attitudes, stimulate involvement, anticipate controversy, or promote voluntary programs of one kind or another, including fund-raising campaigns. Most gatherings of all kinds are for these purposes, and the more they are dramatized, the greater the effect. The deed comes first, and the word comes second. And the essence of the aim is simply to develop confidence.

The state of affairs which these programs seek to affect, it should be noted, is the sum total of an almost infinite number of tremendous trifles: the way telephone calls are handled, the timing and tone of replying to mail, the attitude toward complaints, the reception of visitors, methods of expressing regret and appreciation, and all the other measurements human society has always had for the best people.

Daniel Willard, a momentous mentor of mine in the years 1924–1931, told me there was nothing better for the freight business of the Baltimore & Ohio Railroad than letters of complaint about the food or the service in the dining cars. Mr. Willard had all such letters sent to his desk and handled them himself in such a way as to win many important customers. He was grateful to the kickers; he assured them that under such circumstances he would have been much more upset than they were and made it plain that the thoughtful testimony of such wonderful customers was the best possible help the railroad could have in its constant striving for better service.

Sometimes, of course, particularly with colleges and universities, it is simply not possible to satisfy those who complain. But a certain colleague of mine, in a top role in a top university, long since has had wisdom enough and instinct enough to realize that this is of secondary importance—that what is of the first importance is to pay attention. He answers the letters promptly, and gives them what we have come to call the "two-for-one treatment." If the letter of complaint takes two pages, the answer takes four. His full conversions may be rare, but friends are made, loyalties are reawakened, and the ties of interest and support are almost invariably renewed. Here, I think, is the art of public relations at a high level.

Whoever is in charge, or may hold the impressive titles, the rule for institutions is the same as it is for families: the head of the house is responsible. He does indeed need the best staff help he can get, and is headed for trouble if he tries to get along without it. But it is up to him, and not to any delegated person, to see that the institutional conduct reflects the golden rule, that all designed deeds stay in character, and that the aims truly mirror images that are genuine.

Publicity, on the other hand, is no state of affairs, but an actual and overt function: the communication of information, the pursuit of attention and interest through appeals to eye and ear, and sometimes the natural but unexalted goal of visibility for its own sweet sake. Its routines can be merely good reporting, but its planned aspects have the same basic goal of good public relations programs—building confidence.

It is there, indeed, that the function of publicizing public relations programs gives rise to the popular confusion of terms.

The arts of publicity go back a long way. The ghost writer may be said to have his roots in Genesis 27:22—"The voice is Jacob's voice, but the hands are the hands of Esau." And it was in 1784 that the great Dr. Samuel Johnson reared back and declared, "The trade of advertising is now so near perfection that it is not easy to propose any improvements." And while we now have media unknown in Johnson's time, this giant of the eighteenth century was probably closer to the truth than we might think.

When, for example, has there been any change in the old selling sequence of attention, interest, confidence, desire, and action? When has there been any better way to consider methods of influencing people than the old way of studying people and shaping the plan in light of their likes and fears, their basic motivations, and what they tend to do? All this is in the bones of every good publicity man and comes out at the end of his fingers, in the words of his mouth, and in his moments of quiet and professional meditation.

He admires universality but aims at targets. He knows that publicity in itself raises no money to speak of but that you can't raise money without it. He knows that most people incline toward glimpses and glances rather than studious reading; so he knows too that his message must be told swiftly and in simple terms that catch the eye, warm the heart, and stir the mind. He has a nose for news but little stomach for editorializing. He thinks facts are just fine, especially when they are accurate and easily grasped; but no one knows better than he does that you can't make good succotash out of nothing but lima beans. Above all, perhaps, he plays for dialogue rather than monologue and for repetition rather than single exposure.

He is entitled too, in my opinion, to have it said of him that no one suffers as much as he does because so many of the annual reports of presidents seem to be written primarily for other presidents, printed for younger and more patient eyes, and styled in their layout for times gone by.

Most lay readers today are said to be better schooled in the graphic arts, and it is certainly true that university presses have taken great leaps forward in typography and design. And yet the average annual report in the voluntary field, in the opinion of far too many, is still so steeped in tradition that readers are repelled rather than attracted. And this is a great pity indeed. For as all modern corporations now know so well, the annual report should be the institutional voice at its very best, with every good chance of reaching and influencing the best part of the constituency.

And now for a few odds and ends for publicity people:

If the typography gets more attention than the message, the typography is wrong. And if the format of a printed piece compels a 10-point type size, cut the copy and go no lower than 12-point. On this subject, David M. Church, my friend and colleague for nearly forty years, the first executive director of the American Association of Fund-Raising Counsel, and director of publicity for the National War Fund, suggests that writers and designers should always confer before the typographic patterns have been set. "Never forget," he says, "that the printed word is of paramount importance. Don't let the designer take over and submerge your fine words under a great flood of 'artistic' design. For instance, a full page of solid type with no paragraphs can make a pleasing effect, but who will read it?" (See Appendix 2, "The Least You Should Know about Typography.")

Unless you actually seek hard facts, beware the opinion poll. Face plays a bigger role there than on Mount Rushmore. You either just stir up the comatose negatives, or else all you are apt to get is what they think will make you think they really thought.

The symphonic form is just as good for you as it was for Haydn and Beethoven: "Tell them what you are going to tell them, tell them, and then tell them what you told them."

I used to be a publicity man myself, as the tired saying goes. So I offer this closing fraternal comfort to all curators of the golden words. When you get dog-tired—not from the work, but from what you can't get done—or when people get too stuffy, just remember Mark Twain's inspiring advice: "Always do right. This will gratify some people, and astonish the rest."

Memorial Campaigns

Raising money for some honored name, even when the primary purpose of commemoration also involves a worthy program, is usually a collection rather than a campaign and most of the time results in gifts whose monetary value is about on a level with the cost of funeral wreaths and bouquets.

The phenomenal success of the campaign for the John F. Kennedy Library may have created a contrary popular impression. Actually, it confirms the rules about memorial campaigns rather than contradicts them, and offers fresh evidence of the fundamental requirements for successful fund-raising.

This campaign was a real campaign and had high drama—one of the most visible and shocking tragedies of the century. It had precedent, inasmuch as the people have provided special libraries for all our recent presidents. And best of all—as pointed out to me by the campaign director, James V. Lavin, Boston's solid old pro and my good friend and colleague since National War Fund days—it had "the power and the pipelines."

Within one year of the start on May 16, 1964, the total raised was almost exactly $18,000,000 on a new goal of $21,000,000—stretched from $10,000,000 when the concept of an independent library was broadened to an Institute for Public Administration and Political Science, as a graduate school at Harvard University. And that the other $3,000,000 was going to be raised there seemed to be no doubt.

There were gifts from eight foreign governments, totaling $1,820,000. The number of all gifts was literally enormous, requiring computer aid, but can never be known exactly. Government employees, civilian and military, contributed $2,500,000, but this was counted as one gift. Organized labor, AFL-CIO, pledged $2,000,000, but this too was recorded as one gift only. Almost incredibly, there were some 5,600,000 known gifts of less than $100, and these added up to approximately $2,500,000. There were some 3,700 other gifts and pledges ranging from $100 to $999, totaling "just under" $1,000,000. And it should surprise no experienced fund-raiser to hear that two-thirds of all the money, despite the record-breaking popular response, came in gifts of $1,000 or more. Almost exactly $12,000,000 had been raised by 640 such gifts— 169 of which were for $25,000 or more. The cause was unique. The campaign set new records. But the old laws prevailed.

Without the powerful leverages of this Kennedy memorial, the usual appeals for commemoration would do well to get under way as swiftly as possible and to play up the program part of the case much more than the tribute to the honored name. Especially, I'm sure most of us would say, these appeals should keep an open end on the dollar goals to be sought. Funds that can work either up or down, such as a fund for the purchase of books or for student aid, are preferable here to funds for fixed amounts, involving minimum goals for construction, for endowed professorships, and for any other kind of project for which a shortage would mean failure. The aim of this, of course, is to produce a victory regardless of the number of dollars given.

There are times, of course, when the responsible committee insists upon a special dollar goal. And this is sound enough as fund-raising technique, if only because dollar goals are essential to quotas and giving standards. But in all these cases, there are requirements to be observed with scrupulous care. And a good average model for conducting a memorial appeal in just the right way was the Ed Shea Memorial Scholarship Fund at Princeton, which within a recent year raised $78,222 on a goal of $75,000. David Landman, associate director of development, reported this campaign in a paper for the American College Public Relations Association in July, 1965. Shea, he said, was indeed an exceptional Princetonian— in every important way an outstanding man. But what made the campaign go, he notes, was careful study, group planning, prestigious sponsorship, realistic timing, prospect rating, selective assignments, limited solicitation of a picked constituency for proportionate gifts, report meetings, "passionate advocacy," bulletins at proper intervals, and steady support by attentive staff.

The lessons here should be obvious enough. And the key point to remember is that much as people may revere the past and have love and respect for their friends and their idols, their real concerns are for the future. It does no good to warm the heart if you can't also stir the mind to the right support for bold and useful programs.

Chapter 9

Professional Help: When, Why, and How

$\mathcal{T}$he pressures and problems of current fund-raising, especially for capital purposes, have reached such a stage in the number of programs and the magnitude of goals that the employment of professional counsel for any sort of a major campaign has become a virtual necessity. In any event, in the great majority of such cases the question of professional help should be studied and weighed with the greatest of care.

As a veteran in this field, dating back to 1919, and as one of the organizers and early presidents of the American Association of Fund-Raising Counsel, I ought to know enough to answer the usual inquiries and to say what needs to be said. And I'll promise now that whatever I say will be with as much objectivity as anyone could reasonably expect from a man whose heart has been in this work for some forty-six years and who has found in the field some of the very best of his friends.

Just when do you need outside professionals? What do they do? What are the advantages of employing a professional firm? What plus values are to be expected from the best of them? How are they paid, and for what? And finally, by what criteria should firms be chosen?

In annual campaigns, professional firms are called in either because of successive disappointments without such help, because the cause has no staff people with enough training to direct the appeal, or because only the firm can supply the needed supplementary help. Except for the firms specially geared for church work or for the smaller united funds and community chests, many of the best firms prefer to avoid annual campaigns, and will consent to direct them only for some old client or under genuinely exceptional circumstances.

In capital campaigns, any goal of $50,000 or more should suggest at least considering professional help, though most of the firms would consider a proper minimum to be $100,000. Causes with goals of a million or more should by all means seek the best available aid, unless they are lucky enough, and have been smart enough, to have built up—as at least one big Eastern university has done—a staff of seasoned and successful professionals any top firm would be glad to have.[19]

The time for the employment of a firm should be at the very beginning of things, and not, as the old saying goes, after all the cream has been skimmed off the milk. Any time you wait until you get into trouble, it is very apt to be too late. The doctor has to see the dying man, but the professional fund-raising firm that is doing well—however it may seek to serve the public interest—doesn't have to heed the cries of a really sick campaign. And probably won't.

The function of the professional firm is not to raise the money, but to help you to raise it. And the most important things such a firm does toward that end are in the areas of exploration, goal analysis, planning, direction, records, and keeping things moving. Its first job is to make a plan, based on exploration of the fund-raising potential, with a deliberated judgment on the case, the goal, the requirements for leadership and volunteer help, the timing, the necessary schedule of events, and the necessary cost. The basic task is to plan for the raising of the most money in the least possible time and at the smallest practicable expenditure of effort and cost—within the framework of client policy and within the bounds of good taste. The optimum goal, and the ultimate test of professional skill in planning, is an amount just a little bit more than most people believe can be raised. The good campaign, like the good girdle, has stretch in it.

Doing the things that work, avoiding needless error, and keeping good records are professional functions that should speak for themselves. Most valuable of all, in the opinion of many wise laymen heard over a long period of time, is the function of the catalytic agent—seeing that the right things happen at the right time and that everything keeps rolling right along. And if I may now speak from one of the back pews, let me tell you that this is not always easy.

All professional firms that have won the sanction of their colleagues have certain inherent advantages, and the best of them have a few more advantages that have been hard-won and are beyond price. To begin with, all firms simply have to live in a world of objectivity. For in a field appealing to and depending upon man's very finest emotions, there should be no room or excuse for professional guesswork, hunches, or easy assumptions. One of my clearest memories of my old boss, the late John Price Jones, is of his livid and furious eloquence when anyone used in his presence the very word "assume."

Objectivity comes more easily to firms, if only because their staffs are immune to the payroll pressures that often handicap those who work directly for the institution and who for that reason have to go away or let up when the head man says he's tired.

Firms of any standing, aside from their obvious experience, have the standard practices, the answers for all the stock negatives, the "book" on the data, the gift tables, check lists, and other tools, ways of comparing the time schedules, records on comparative costs, etc. And because they render a group service, they offer too a valuable kind of staff insurance against the almost inevitable perils of individual illness, unexpected resignations, and suddenly revealed incompetence. All firms, let us observe, also enjoy the common experience that their men are initially accepted as experts—if only as prophets away from home.

The best of the firms have important plus values. Candor may be the first of these, providing the assurance that you can always count on them to lay it on the line. This alone can be mighty important to presiding administrators, for as Harold Dodds has pointed out, administrative assistants can become far too expert in "the arts of incomplete disclosure."

Top supervision is another plus value—regular visitation by a senior officer of the firm for a checkup on the job and the personnel, invariably helpful both to the firm's own staff and its clients and, to my way of thinking, one of the real hallmarks of any firm's quality. And this usually carries with it a process of continuous diagnosis which uncovers troubles a little faster and gets quicker remedial action.

And then too the better firms are more likely to do a superior job in helping to train the institution's own personnel, and in the ever-mounting task, as national goals keep climbing, of seeking and training the extra staff now needed for field work and field offices. That this is getting to be a matter of real magnitude is evidenced by the staff statistics for several big capital campaigns completed within the past few years: Harvard had 74—31 management and 43 clerical; Princeton had 66—30 management and 36 clerical; and the Massachusetts Institute of Technology had 79—28 management and 51 clerical. No firm ever supplies more than a few key people. The other temporary help has to be found, and is usually put on the institution's own payroll. Rarer than rubies the really good people are, and it takes a ruby hunter to find them.

The better firms are more likely too to leave behind them a sound and workable blueprint for the future. And because they are the best, with all the independence and professional pride that goes with it, they will usually insist on the observance of proper sequences and other fundamentals, and all the more so when pressed to take short cuts. They focus their concerns on the affairs of their clients and waste no time fretting about credit. For these are the wise who have been around long enough to know that "to seek credit is to lose it, and that to disclaim credit is usually to get more than you probably deserve."

All firms worth having are paid a fee, and never a percentage. And their charges are based on the number of men assigned, the duration of the service, and the out-of-pocket expenses involved. Fees for the exploration job and the planning may be figured separately—particularly if the findings are negative, which happens more often than you might suppose, and the proposed campaign has to be canceled or postponed. But the fee for campaign service will be at the rate agreed upon in advance, win, lose, or draw. Some part of this fee, it should be pointed out, will be an expense to the cause whether or not professional help is employed, for the cost of the extra people on the campaign payroll. Figures can be cited showing that the total cost of campaigns professionally directed has been less than comparable campaigns without such outside help, but my opinion is that such data are of secondary importance and of doubtful relevance. Campaigns are much more likely to get into trouble by not spending enough money than they are by spending too much.

How many firms there are in the business of fund-raising nobody seems to know. But there are twenty-eight firms which are members of the American Association of Fund-Raising Counsel and which for that reason have passed stiff tests and have agreed to observe a rigorous code, shown on page 177. So that is as good a place as any to start looking.[12]

Your choice can be narrowed initially by a few purely factual considerations. Only a few firms are complete specialists, doing nothing, say, but hospital work or church campaigns. Some firms are largely regional in their scope and experience, and very few have had extensive experience in New York City. Some firms are geared to do a remarkably fast job on certain types of community campaigns, and others are accustomed to a duration of service measured in years. Performance records will show what sort of causes the firms usually serve and at what goal levels. All such data are relevant.

But because you will need most of all the establishment of confidence, you need first to be satisfied about the men now running the firm, the men they propose to assign, and the general system by which their service is rendered. The firm's history may be impressive, but the relevant question for you and your cause is what the firm has done recently in your field and for comparable goals and similar institutions. The current people are the prime factor in your choice—who will do the exploration and the planning, who will do the supervising,

Fair Practice Code of the American Association of Fund-Raising Counsel, Inc.[20]

One. Member firms will serve only those charitable institutions or agencies whose purposes and methods they can approve. They will not knowingly be used by any organization to induce charitably inclined persons to give their money to unworthy causes.

Two. Member firms do business only on the basis of a specified fee, determined prior to the beginning of the campaign. They will not serve clients on the unprofessional basis of a percentage or commission of the sums raised. They maintain this ethical standard also by not profiting, directly or indirectly, from disbursements for the accounts of clients.

Three. The executive head of a member organization must demonstrate at least a six-year record of continuous experience as a professional in the fund-raising field. This helps to protect the public from those who enter the profession without sufficient competence, experience, or devotion to ideals of public service.

Four. The Association looks with disfavor upon firms which use methods harmful to the public, such as making exaggerated claims of past achievements, guaranteeing results, and promising to raise unobtainable sums.

Five. No payment in cash or kind shall be made by a member to an officer, director, trustee, or advisor of a philanthropic agency or institution as compensation for using his influence for the engaging of a member for fund-raising counsel.

and who will be the senior man on the job, directing your campaign. Your own impressions on these points should be checked with others, and not by quoted testimony or by correspondence, but always in person or by phone. Getting out the microscope is being none too cautious.

You might, of course, go outside the ranks of the association in your choice of firm and do so with good results. But beware of any firm, inside or out of any recognized group, that promises a painless or easy effort, talks payment on a contingency or percentage basis, or makes what sounds even faintly like excessive claims. And any firm that says it never had a failure is either a blatant liar or else is just starting up in business.

One other thing about the process of selection. When you get down to a relatively small list of firms to be considered, my advice is to see them in their own offices. But if you wish for some good reason to see them at the site of the institution, it would be well to avoid one of those nonstop performances like Atlantic City's annual choice of Miss America, the quiz contest, competitive bidding, instant character analysis, and all the rest of it. You don't pick lawyers and doctors that way, and fund-raising firms don't like it either. If they know something of that sort is going to happen, some of the better firms won't put up with it at all. They just won't come.

Some of the firms do consulting work, and then there are consultants who never direct campaigns. Either way, it should be remembered that the most important function of consultation is not to play the wizard, but simply to provide at stated intervals the perspective that is possible only with triangulation. Perspective in turn leads to confidence, and confidence is the one biggest thing in the whole fund-raising process—always worth taking plenty of pains to find.

Chapter **10**

Leadership
Should Have
Two Dimensions

*J*ust as any good pair of scissors needs two blades, with each blade helping to keep the other sharp, so it is that any good fund-raising operation needs both kinds of leadership—the layman who leads and the staff man who manages and serves. The better each is and the better they work together, the better the result will be. And leadership in itself, let it never be forgotten, is always the key factor in successful fund-raising, whatever the cause, whatever the goal, and whatever the scope of the campaign.

The old pros know a lot about this, through their long joys and sorrows, but there are always the young staff members coming up, who need to know as rapidly as possible what their standards should be and how to work well with others. And then there are the come-and-go laymen too, most of whom should find profit and pleasure in knowing more about the professionals and what the respective relationships ought to be.

So my aims in this final chapter, in the interest of helping people to understand each other better and thus work better together, are (1) to review the makings of a good pro, (2) to suggest to newcomers in the professional field how to build up their status and improve their skills, (3) to speak briefly of the basic relationship between professional staff and the supervising laity, (4) to suggest what the laity should expect and look for in the staff of people who serve them, and (5) to remind everybody what the big satisfactions are when all goes well.

Hallmarks of the Good Pro

Those of us in the voluntary field have no better compliment for any colleague than to say he is a good pro. And by that we don't mean merely that he makes his living that way and is competent. What we mean primarily is that he thinks and acts like a dedicated professional—with poise, stability, perspective, and proper respect for the rules and traditions of his craft. His hallmarks are simple, easy to discern, and worth noting.

Poise probably comes first, because a pro's first duty is to help generate an atmosphere of confidence in the cause he serves, in the professional part of the job, in his colleagues, or—if he is in the fund-raising business—in his firm. To do this takes an obviously genuine attitude that can make the difference, for example, between real and communicable enthusiasm and mere excitability, or the difference between warmth and mere heat. A pro with poise avoids getting on the defensive and is hospitable to so-called "new ideas." He admits error promptly and cheerfully and personally assumes the blame. He realizes that a "crisis" is usually a tiresome repetition of some old script. He has capacity for indignation about the right things but rarely loses his temper. He bears the burdens of modesty as well as he can but treasures his own self-respect. He knows the distinction between accomplishment and mere activity and apportions his time and energies accordingly.

The good pro also has something related to poise, which might as well be termed stability. He tries to get his feet down on solid ground by habitually asking himself questions like these: "Do I really know what I'm doing or supposed to do? Have I all the facts I need? All the pertinent opinion? What has the previous experience been? Can this position be defended, and explained clearly?"

He heeds honest impulse when long years justify it, but he tries hard never to act on impulse alone. For well he knows, as all the good seniors know, that shooting from the hip misses many targets, pleases few people, and engenders more distrust than confidence.

Respect for the time factor is another hallmark. The good pro knows that every pickle has to soak a while, and therefore he insists, however importunate others may be, on allowing for enough soak time. He bewares of short cuts, has respect for established sequences, and is well aware that campaigns, like mice and elephants, have their own periods of gestation, rarely subject to change.

Professionals develop perspective through experience. By training, emulation, and more often by trial and error, they learn to weigh things relatively, never forgetting the law of diminishing returns or where the money is. They know there is never enough staff or enough good volunteers, and they don't fret about it. They merely ask themselves, "How important is it? How productive is it likely to be, taking into account the time and cost involved and other possible moves?" They know that the further the campaign periphery is extended, the less productive the result, and that banks don't count percentage of participation, just money. They respect and admire eloquence and all the good uses of publicity and the printed word, but what they seek most of all is the kind of action and dynamics that leads informed and dedicated laymen into fruitful conversations. Only by keeping his own sense of perspective in ways such as these can the good pro persuade others to pay more attention to priorities and deadlines.

Finally, and vitally, the seasoned professional respects his vocation, his colleagues, and all good work done in his field. He has a genuine sense of mission and both the ability and the desire to see the cause he serves in a good and shining light.

So much for the professional prototype. And if not many have all those virtues, you may still be assured that these are the hallmarks all the best men recognize and strive for. But for the trainees and newcomers—now coming into the field by the hundreds—there are other things to be said.

Suggestions for Newcomers and Trainees. It may seem needlessly elementary, but it is worth reminding recruits about xenophobia—fear of the stranger. Too much difference from expected or normal standards, in matters of dress, comportment, habits of speech, knife and fork drill, and so on, will at the least be distracting, and at the worst can upset confidence. Some of us remember one colleague, for instance, whose ties and socks spoke with such insistent fervor that we could hardly concentrate on the words of his mouth.

Blending yourself quietly into the background, at any rate, is a good rule to start with.

The first of my operating suggestions to newcomers, and perhaps the best, is to acquire quickly the habit of being ever watchful for the tremendous trifles. Find out, for example, all you can that is pertinent about the people you are to work with: date and place of birth, the old home town if it was elsewhere, school and college classes and activities, honors, hobbies, board memberships, religion, family data, political affiliations, clubs, fraternal orders, and particularly any odd preferences or special phobias. All this can come in handy, in more ways than you may suppose, and can certainly keep you out of trouble. (Old-timers of some thirty-five years ago may remember one important chairman with whom it was almost suicidal to use the word "contact" as a verb.)

Other weighty trifles are such things as determining your chairman's best and worst conference days and hours, his tastes in correspondence, his leanings in the area of semantics, and above all the way he likes to have his name spelled. By all means get to know the secretaries and how to enlist their aid—in such ways, for instance, as seeing to it that your phone messages, memos, or notes are up near the top of the pile, and not down at the bottom. Keep your watch on time, and never see a layman without an agenda in plain sight. And then—because it helps to create confidence, save time, and make for a nice state of euphoria—always take notes. Taking notes doesn't necessarily turn casual remarks into deathless utterances, but has never been known to evoke open displeasure. And if you don't take notes, your average layman is certain to feel vaguely troubled—to wonder whether you are going to remember all he said, whether your visit is mere routine, and all that sort of thing.

Next to the tremendous trifles, always at the heart of public relations, and especially personal relations, I would recommend the stretch toward the unexpected, something lifetime clerks never seem to heed. It is all very well to do competently what you are paid to do. That is always expected and taken for granted. But it must go away back to the Medes and Persians to say that the big hits and the long jumps come from what you do beyond the assignment and beyond the conventional time.

As an important example of extra effort with sure rewards, I would strongly recommend learning more about writing. Pamphlets and other formal material may be for the specialist, but as long as many faculties keep on regarding English composition as a mere tool subject not worthy of much teaching, the art of simple communication will continue to find itself in trouble. Few can attain real style or eloquence. But all can at least aim for clarity, grace, vigor, and brevity, the four prose virtues taught by Frederick C. Packard, Jr., now retired, to all class orators at Harvard from 1925 to 1965.

If you would write to please and persuade—certainly part of your job—see also what Benjamin Franklin had to say in the early pages of his *Autobiography* about the Socratic method of argument. This will help you to write "You may be interested" instead of "You will be interested," and could save you from getting into rhetorical habits that are overly dogmatic and irritatingly positive. *The Elements of Style,* by William Strunk, Jr., and E. B. White, is another little book you should consult regularly, whether or not you aspire to be a top writer.

Eschew the big and fancy words, young brothers and sisters; stay away from the meaningless and inexact words like "many" and those endemic clichés like "crystal" clear, "perfected" plans, and "highly trained" staff. Beware the marathon sentence and the tiresome paragraph, and don't forget that not all of those four-letter words are nasty words. Keep it simple, to be sure, but let even brevity have its heartbeat. Statistics alone are for computers; what you say and write can be as objective as you please, but the big aim has to be to please and persuade. (See accompanying check list for copy review.)

The "rough draft" should be avoided, unless actually requested or unless the specifications were obscure. For why shouldn't you do the best you can before submitting it to others? And then when you do submit copy of any kind, make the tactful and gracious allowance for possible changes by saying "For comment or suggestions," instead of the cocky and presumptuous "For your OK." Never resent comment and criticism, incidentally; go looking for it. For English in our field is not written, but rewritten. In fact, you can take it from one whose own prose attempts have been knocked around more than he would like to remember that most of the copy that goes through unscathed is copy that comes out unsung.

It seems pertinent to add that the careful pro proofreads his own mail, and especially mail intended for lay signatures, and almost never asks a secretary to sign his name. Similarly, when he puts in a call to any layman or any pro of higher rank, he gets on the phone himself before the call is completed. (John D. Rockefeller, Jr., used to do this and then compound the astonishment by simply saying, "This is John Rockefeller." So who are we?)

I would stress too the odd fact that the individual fares best not as the star performer, but as a proud and loyal member of a team. Your views will carry more weight with a

CHECK LIST FOR COPY REVIEW: BROCHURES, PAMPHLETS, ETC.

Writers would make things far easier for those who have to review and approve their copy if they were to attach a memorandum covering such points as these:

Purpose. What is this piece supposed to accomplish? Where does it fit in the general plan, and why?

Audience. What elements of the constituency are to get this? How much do they know about the case and about the institution? What is their feeling of responsibility likely to be? Which of their possible interests will be paramount?

Probable Format. Is the piece intended for typewritten appearance only, or is it to be printed? If to be printed, about what size, about how many pages? Is there to be art work, so that captions can tell part of the story? Is the piece intended for the library table or the pocket of a worker?

Probable Distribution. Is it for mass mailing, for selective mailing with a covering letter, or for distribution by the hand of volunteers?

Promotional Possibilities. Is any part of the piece intended for condensed use in the institutional magazine? Is all or part of it to be given to speakers? Are certain paragraphs to be used in letters or in manuals for workers? In general, what uses are possible or contemplated?

Missing Data. If the piece is now incomplete, what is missing, and when will the data become available? What committee names are to be appended, and what address for those who may ask for further information?

group judgment behind them. More confidence will be built by reminders that you have behind you good colleagues who gladly share the problems and help find the solutions. And don't worry about making mistakes. If nothing else, they show you are up there swinging. At best, as your wise seniors will tell you, occasional error can sometimes lead to confidence more quickly than unblemished accomplishment. Don't worry either if there are things you don't know. Never try to bluff about it, for you can always make a hit by saying frankly that you don't know, but will try to find out.

All professionals, as a matter of fact, do better by taking the position that there are some things nobody knows much about, other things on which the other man's opinion is just as good as theirs, but a few things about which the answers are certain and open to no shadow of doubt—no possible doubt whatever. This paves the way for the good pro to be as dogmatic as he pleases in his insistence on fundamentals and his rejection of the unsound. And on the other hand, people will be much more likely to hate you than follow you if you try to pretend that you are right all the time.

Students in this field and newcomers to operating ranks should never let it worry them that the layman is the boss. For as the Pentagon knows and as Henry Wriston pointed out in that delightfully illuminating book of his, *Academic Procession,* experts are generally subject to supervision by amateurs. And the task of the expert, he says, is to educate the amateurs and find work for them to do. This, I submit, is the truth with comfort, carrying plenty of kudos for all. (As a postscript here, may I say that most of the old pros eschew the "expert" image—not for the reason cited by Dr. Wriston, but simply because the more any man deserves to be rated that way, the more he becomes aware of his ignorance.)

Basic Relationship between Professional Staff and Supervising Laity

Summarizing these comments about professionals, old and new, it should be admitted and duly recognized that voluntary agencies run the constant risk of becoming too professionalized. And yet they need the most competent help they can get. Therein lies the perennial dilemma of the professional group: how to follow the subtle line between the policy and the leadership that should be the layman's and the management that should be the staff's. That line is best observed when the professional seeks always the first-class counsel of first-class laymen.

In turn, the layman will do well to remember that cheap help is the most expensive help and that the best investment any agency can make, at almost any price, is an investment in top staff—people with integrity, stability, loyalty, and common sense.

Thoughtful laymen will understand staff people a little better, and how staff people operate, by coming to understand a few of their basic attitudes. Their motivations are essentially altruistic. They certainly seek neither power nor riches. Their positions are now rewarded much better than they used to be, perhaps as belated justice but more likely as the beneficent workings of the laws of supply and demand. But their jobs are still relatively insecure, unrecognized, and unsung. The best of them put program first, where it should be, and play for the long haul rather than immediacy. The honorable career means more to them than any temporary triumph. They are used to working with top people, so they are not easy to impress. And they are not easy to budge, for the valuable reason that they have been there before, and know what they are doing.

The first things a layman has a right to expect from the staff are a plan, a schedule, and a budget. And then he has a right to expect candor, consideration, ethical practices, loyalty, periodic and objective reports, and hopefully all the little niceties that go with personal service work at its best. And then I'll say it separately to gain the added emphasis: the layman should and must expect the unrelenting exertion of sensible pressure and polite but firm insistence on the tested laws and sequences of fund-raising. For as Frank J. Goodnow, when president of Johns Hopkins University, said once to his trustees in my youthful presence, "Well, gentlemen, if you're going to hire a watchdog, what's the use of doing your own barking?"

Finally—and what a great word that is, my countrymen! —staff people and laymen alike should remember occasionally for their own comfort and self-respect that theirs is a function which perforce is always in a position of advocating higher standards and optimum performance. They are thus advancing the common welfare and the common culture as few others are ever privileged to do. In this way, as Justice Frankfurter suggested, they are making civilization the real business of the United States.

Perhaps that is what John R. Mott, the great evangelical leader of the YMCA, had in mind when he said, "Blessed are the money-raisers. For in Heaven they shall stand next to the martyrs."

Appendixes

APPENDIX 1. CHECK LISTS FOR FUND-RAISING ESSENTIALS AND SEQUENCES

Essentials:

Campaign	Public relations	Publicity	Direct mail
Case	Participation	What?	Personalize
Leadership	Recognition	Where?	Dramatize
Workers	Optimism	When?	Popularize
Prospects	Universality	Who?	Particularize
Dynamics	Dramatization	How?	Follow up

Sequences:

Basic procedure	Selling	Special presentations	Campaign
Definition	Attention	Problem	Planning
Investigation	Interest	Proposal	Preparation
Analysis	Confidence	Cost	Organization
Production	Conviction	Opportunity	Indoctrination
Evaluation	Desire		Rating
Records	Action		Advance gifts
			Opening
			Formal drive
			Cleanup
			Records

APPENDIX 2. THE LEAST YOU SHOULD KNOW ABOUT TYPOGRAPHY

You can't have organized fund-raising without printed literature. And you can't have printed literature without getting involved in at least a few of the mysteries of typography.

Because readers here almost invariably have to be coaxed, the two big essentials are (1) that the printed material must be easy to read, especially for the older people with fatter purses but weaker eyes, and (2) that it should conform generally with established tastes and reading habits. Otherwise, readers are likely to be either distracted or repelled—and the printed literature will then be worse than a total loss, evoking irritation as well as failing to win its desired audience.

Some printers are good printers but mediocre typographers. Some typographers may be ever so daring and inventive, but know little about the problems of persuading the myopic or reluctant reader. So the best thing to do is to find a printer whose previous production indicates he knows good typography or knows how to get it. If your campaign is a big one, seeking big gifts, it may pay to retain a consulting typographer, competent to make sure your printed material is attractive, readable, in good taste, in character with the cause, and suited to your audiences.

Most of the time, for instance, you will want to use book or antique paper, like this, but sometimes glossy or coated paper may be better. Should the piece be done by letterpress or by offset? If illustrations are to be used, what kind, and where? You may wish to distinguish all your printed matter by some kind of distinctive art work. On some pieces color may be important—enough but not too much. You can't afford to create an impression of sheer lavishness or reckless luxury, but neither can you afford to look skimpy or cheap. These are some of the more significant reasons why it is perilous for amateurs to play expert and why the best typographic advice you can get is never too good.

Proportions

The sizes and dimensions of your printed material must be flexible, and their aim should begin with the inside pocket of a man's jacket, never straying far from the fundamental that most of the printed material in organized fund-raising should be carried by workers rather than sent by mail. The more important the piece, indeed, the closer it should come to a conversation aid—an attractive guide to dialogue.

But even though you defer in such matters to the established expert, as you should, I have always thought it both helpful and interesting to know something about the old and basic laws of good proportion.

The ideal length and width, for example, is still the golden rectangle, as it was when the Greeks designed the Parthenon. Its ratio is 1:1.6, which translated to the printed page means that width is not less than two-thirds, or more than three-quarters, of the up-and-down measurement. This comes out, for example, at a comfortable average of 7¼ by 10. And variations of the same proportion are easily found along a diagonal line drawn on such a page. (Come down 7 inches to the diagonal, and you'll have a width of 5 inches.)

The optical center, useful to know for the location of titles and key art, is about three-eighths of the way down, which should make it 3¾ inches from the top on a page 7¼ by 10. (The exact center, you will find, always looks too low.)

White space in most pamphlets should take up anywhere from about 50 per cent of the page in large brochures to about 30 per cent in leaflets and fact cards.

Magazine people usually don't like subheads, but fund-raising literature often needs them. Academicians relish lengthy paragraphs, it seems, but for purposes of coaxing readers any paragraph of as many as ten lines may be a wee bit too long.

Type Design

The wider the line, the larger the type size should be. For larger pamphlets 12-point type (72 points to the vertical inch) should be considered a probable minimum, and 14-point would be much more likely to woo the fading eye. Anything smaller than 10-point type on a 12-point base could be fatal. And one more warning: if the copy is too long for the design, cut the copy—don't ever go to smaller type just to make it fit.

People are used to reading books and magazines. Which means they are not accustomed to much type which is either in italics or all in capital letters. "Upper and lower," as they say in the trade, and as the type appears here, is the stuff to feed most readers.

For the same reason, conservative type faces are considered preferable to anything noticeably "different." (Always avoid sheer distraction and the needless challenge to xenophobia.)

Note. If you must read proof, which the careful pros always do and the responsible laymen usually should, ask your printer for a copy of proofreaders' marks. And you'll save money by not forgetting that printer's corrections are on the house but author's corrections are on you.

APPENDIX 3. CLASSIC QUOTES PERTINENT TO FUND-RAISING

From the Bible

Ask, and it shall be given you; seek, and ye shall find. *Matthew 7:7; Luke 11:9*

For whosoever hath, to him shall be given. *Matthew 13:12; Luke 8:18*

Let your light so shine before men that they may see your good works. *Matthew 5:16*

If a man is willing to give, the value of his gift is in its proportion to what he has, not to what he has not. *II Corinthians 8, Goodspeed translation*

For if the trumpet give an uncertain sound, who shall prepare himself to the battle? *I Corinthians 14:8*

For the Planners

Make no little plans. They have no magic to stir men's blood and probably themselves will not be realized. Make big plans; aim high in hope and work, remembering that a noble, logical diagram once recorded will never die, but long after we are gone will be a living thing, asserting itself with ever-growing insistency. Remember that our sons and grandsons are going to do things that would stagger us. Let your watchword be order and your beacon beauty. Think big. *Daniel Burnham*

It is unwise to pay too much, but worse to pay too little. When you pay too much, you lose a little money. That is all. But when you pay too little, you sometimes lose all, because the thing you bought was incapable of doing the thing it was bought to do. The common law of business balance prohibits paying *little* and getting a *lot*. It can't be done. If you deal with the lowest bidder, it is well to add something for the risk you run. And if you do that you will have enough to pay for something better.   *John Ruskin*

Much I learned from my teachers—more from my friends, and most of all from my pupils.   *Rabbi Hillel*

For the Volunteer

Nothing but what you volunteer has the essence of life, the springs of pleasure in it. These are the things you do because you want to do them, the things your spirit has chosen for its satisfaction. . . .

The more you are stimulated to such action the more clearly does it appear to you that you are a sovereign spirit, put into the world, not to wear harness, but to work eagerly without it. *Woodrow Wilson, baccalaureate address at Princeton, June 13, 1909*

It is one of the most beautiful compensations of life that no man can sincerely try to help another without helping himself.   *Ralph Waldo Emerson*

Great messages make the messenger great. ("Who am I?" asked Moses. And the Lord said, "You speak for me.")

For All Solicitors

Some people have a less keen sense of their duty and responsibility than others. With them a little urging may be helpful. But with most people a convincing presentation of the facts and the need is far more effective. When a solicitor comes to you and lays on your heart the responsibility that rests so heavily on his; when his earnestness gives convincing evidence of how seriously interested he is; when he makes it clear that he knows you are no less anxious to do your duty in the matter than he is, that you are just as conscientious, that he feels sure all you need is to realize the importance of the enterprise and the urgency of the need in order to lead you to do your full share in meeting it,—he has made you his friend and has brought you to think of giving not as a duty but as a privilege. *John D. Rockefeller, Jr.*

For Curators of the Golden Words

Everything has been said. But as no one listens, everything has to be said again. *André Gide*

It is not so relevant whether you are right or wrong, but it is cardinal that you should be positive. *C. P. Snow, Godkin lectures at Harvard*

I have made this letter rather long only because I have not had time to make it shorter. *Pascal, Lettres Provinciales, 1656*

Being right is not enough—you have to be believed, and without causing irritation. . . .

It is not good Public Relations to cater to Public Opinion. *Henry M. Wriston*

For the Intolerant

The spirit of liberty is the spirit which is not too sure that it is right.

The spirit of liberty is the spirit which seeks to understand the minds of other men and women. The spirit of liberty is the spirit which weighs their interests alongside its own without bias. *Judge Learned Hand*

Let me remind you, gentlemen, that academic freedom involves the right to be wrong as well as the right to be right. *Nicholas Murray Butler*

For the Fainthearted

Don't ever dare to take your College as a matter of course—because, like democracy and freedom, many people you'll never know anything about have broken their hearts to get it for you.   *Alice Duer Miller, at a dinner celebrating the fiftieth anniversary of Barnard College, 1939*

There may be somebody who . . . doubts the generosity and the spirit of this great city. Be assured that when the campaign is over, we can go to him and say what Henry IV said to his General, "Go hang yourself, brave Crillon; we have won a great victory and you were not there!"   *Mrs. Dwight W. Morrow*

You never know how far you can reach until you stretch. *Anonymous*

For the Prophets of Impending Doom

Our earth is degenerate in these latter days. Bribery and corruption are common. Children no longer obey their parents. Every man wants to write a book. . . . The end of the world is evidently approaching.   *On a stone slab carved in 2800 B.C., in Assyria*

It is a gloomy moment in history. Not for many years . . . has there been so much . . . apprehension. . . . Never has the future seemed so incalculable. . . . In France the political caldron seethes. . . . Russia hangs . . . like a cloud . . . on the horizon. . . . All the . . . resources . . . of the British Empire are sorely tried. . . . Of our own troubles [in the United States] no man can see the end.   *Harper's Weekly, October 10, 1857*

APPENDIX 4. RECOMMENDED READINGS

This appendix is not a bibliography, and some of the titles listed for background are out of print. But copies should be in libraries, and all of them are worthy of reading, review, and reference. [21]

For Better Background

Philanthropic Foundations, by F. Emerson Andrews, Russell Sage Foundation, New York, 1956.

> Here, surely, is Mr. Foundation himself. With the Russell Sage Foundation from 1928 to 1956 and since then the director of the Foundation Library Center in New York City, this definitive authority has probably done more writing and made more speeches about foundations and their practices than anyone of ordinary zeal would think possible. I picked the above choice among his seven volumes for its date and target. But I should add that his *Foundation Directory,* edition I, 1964, also belongs on the shelves in any fund-raising library.

The Academic President: Educator or Caretaker? by Harold W. Dodds, McGraw-Hill Book Company, New York, 1962.

> Distinguished leader and administrator himself in his long years as president of Princeton, Mr. Dodds presents here a distillation of administrative experience in a wide variety of institutions in all parts of the country. Though necessarily keyed to education, his findings and observations are applicable to all sorts of voluntary bodies. With thoughtful reading, this Dodds book should help fund-raisers to understand better the traditions and frameworks within which they must learn to operate if relationships are to be harmonious, effective, and memorable.

Corporation Giving in a Free Society, by Richard Eels, Harper & Row, Publishers, Incorporated, New York, 1956.

> This pioneering study of the social and economic aspects of business philanthropy reflects the thoughts of top corporate officers and the leadership of top corporations. There are several books about corporate giving, but this volume by Mr. Eels carries the recommendation of authorities who know this field far better than I do. Just remember as you read that this area of philanthropy, especially for education and even more so for religious causes, is relatively unexplored.

The True Believer, by Eric Hoffer, Harper & Row, Publishers, Incorporated, New York, 1951. (Also available in a paperback edition as a Mentor Book, New American Library of World Literature, Inc., New York.)

This classic study of fanaticism is a triumph of serendipity if I ever saw one —a really great example of how to learn obliquely. Turn Hoffer's negatives into positives, and substitute constructive leadership for his Hitlers and other rascals—in effect, read with a mirror in your hand—and you'll have a wealth of data and wisdom useful in fund-raising or in any other field involving the arts of persuasion. You'll understand lots of things better, have fewer fears, and waste less time on fruitless endeavors after you have read and studied this fascinating book.

Philanthropy's Role in Civilization, by Arnaud C. Marts, Harper & Row, Publishers, Incorporated, New York, 1953.

My friend and colleague for more than thirty years, Arnaud Marts has won his honors in many fields. But the rest of us like to think of him as a leader and senior statesman in professional fund-raising. He helped establish and lend character to the American Association of Fund-Raising Counsel, and by word and deed has always done more than his share to equate fund-raising at its best with the advancement of all good things. Among several of his books, I recommend this particular volume for background and vision.

Fund-Raising for Higher Education, by John A. Pollard, Harper & Row, Publishers, Incorporated, New York, 1958.

Dr. Pollard, vice-president of the Council for Financial Aid to Education, which fosters support by corporations, is the student, analyst, and interpreter who lends substance to its program and scholarly integrity to its positions and publications. I suggest this volume of his because it concerns itself with fund-raising for education far more extensively than was physically possible in this book of mine. And even if I had had the space, John's book contains material I would almost certainly have missed.

Academic Procession, by Henry M. Wriston, Columbia University Press, New York, 1959.

Mr. Wriston's renown, of course, was won as an educator; and he was indeed a good one. But in addition to all those fruitful years at Wesleyan, Lawrence, and Brown, he won early spurs as a fund-raiser and almost three decades later went to the top in that field as president of the Rhode Island War Chest and as a key member of the executive committee of the National War Fund. This particular book of his, I assure you, is far broader than its title. Anyone who is doing any kind of administrative work or who has to work with administrators should have the fun and rewards of reading it. Once you start, you'll find it hard to put it down, happily collecting aphoristic gems as you glide smoothly along through the captivating Wriston prose.

For Current Trends and Statistics[22]

Giving USA, by the American Association of Fund-Raising Counsel, Inc., 500 Fifth Avenue, New York, New York 10036.

This annual handbook, available on request, abounds with current statistics and data on the various areas of philanthropy, on the sources of giving, and on the rules and membership of the association itself. (See also the association's fairly frequent *Bulletin,* and *Philanthropic Digest,* by John Price Jones Company, Inc.)

Acknowledgments

For anyone writing a book only once in a long while and taking some years to do it, the pleasant duty of making acknowledgments eludes easy definition. Where does it start, and where does it end?

Generally, I feel a vast debt for all I have learned from so many fellow professionals in this relatively new field of ours, which David McCord tells me John Buchan once called "this noble merchantry of civilization." And I am thankful too, as all honest professionals should be, to all the good laymen I have worked with, for what they too have taught me.

But specifically, as in all dilemmas, choices have to be made, both in topic selection and in the planning and preparation of copy, and then in resolving my own initial doubts about whether enough people would really want to read a book like this and want to own a copy.

First to mind come David M. Church, Carl A. Kersting, and his son Donald L. Kersting—old friends and good pros who stood by with helping hands so patiently and carefully during the many long months of literary gestation. Here too, at times when I needed it most, I had the expert help of my Tenafly neighbor, F. Emerson Andrews, president of the Foundation Library Center of New York. And I am indebted too to Herbert S. Bailey, Jr., director and editor of the Princeton University Press, who in the critical eleventh hour gave me fresh encouragement and many a fine suggestion.

Special parts of this book were reviewed and beefed up by other old friends, as noted in the text. But I don't know where to stop.

All I can say, to everybody who helped on the copy job and to all who permitted me to quote them, is that they have my lasting thanks.

On the other question that loomed so large for me, about the possible demand for this book, I saw no way to find a dependable answer except to ask friends for a show of hands—even though I had nothing at that time to display but a bare Table of Contents.

The hands went up, and with influential advocacy and impressive example. Edna Geissler, director of financial-resources development for the YWCA, showed what national organizations might do. Jess Speidel, vice-president of the American Cancer Society, demonstrated what the demand might be among national health agencies. And another old friend, Carlton Ketchum, president of Ketchum, Inc., and a genuine leader among professional fund-raising executives for more than forty years, came up quickly with evidence that in the fund-raising business itself there was a substantial market.

Most of all in this connection, special thanks are due the American Alumni Council and the Association of American Colleges. The council's executive director, George J. Cooke, Jr., offered substantial encouragement from the very beginning, culminating in the generous support of the Tracy Foundation, of Arizona, which enabled the council to distribute the book as a service to its fund-raising membership.

And it was two other old friends, successive chairmen of the Association, who led unanimous board action for sending copies to all member institutions: Rosemary Park, president of Barnard College, and Bishop James P. Shannon, president of the College of St. Thomas. This act of theirs, together with what the council had done and the evidence brought forth by those other old friends, gave the project all the practical encouragement anyone could reasonably ask.

Once again the old truth shines out that there's nothing quite like the warm words and stout backing of good friends. All of them, I hardly need say, have my·enduring appreciation.

Harold J. Seymour

Annotations

to the Second Edition

In the almost quarter-century between the first and second editions of this book, the fund-raising field has grown and changed tremendously. But Harold J. Seymour's basic insights into philanthropy, people, and fund-raising are as brilliant and helpful today as when he first wrote them. In 1988, Charles E. Lawson, chairman and CEO of Brakeley, John Price Jones Inc., studied the 1966 text with an expert eye, noting the statistics and practices that had changed significantly between editions. His annotations follow. They are numbered, and those numbers also appear in the appropriate positions of the main text, which remains exactly as Mr. Seymour wrote it.

1. (page xv) — In 1987, philanthropic giving in the United States alone totaled $93.68 billion. An estimated 48 per cent of the population served as volunteers. And, about 422,000 organizations had 501(c)(3) status, which enabled them to receive tax deductible gifts.

2. (page xv) — Currently, individuals are giving 2.05 per cent of personal income to charity.

3. (pages 5 & 33) — The "rule of three" held for many years. However, more recent experience now indicates a possible "40-40-20" rule — 40 per cent of the campaign total will come from the top 10 gifts, the next 40 per cent from the following 100 gifts and the last 20 per cent from

everybody else. These are guidelines for big-gift campaigns rather than for large annual efforts.

4. (page 25) — In 1987, individual giving as a portion of personal income was 2.05 per cent, considerably lower than the level implied by Mr. Seymour. (The difference can be largely explained by improved accuracy in assembling and reporting data on philanthropy.) The same year, corporations gave about 1.6 per cent of pre-tax net income, 8.4 per cent less than the 10 per cent the law currently allows to be deducted.

5. (pages 38 & 62) — The computer and word processing have made "carding" prospects almost extinct. Today's fund-raising staff can manage a volume of prospects and data far beyond the capability of the manual systems available to Mr. Seymour's contemporaries.

6. (page 51) — See note 3. Initially, either the "rule of three" or "40-40-20" can be a good basis for testing the final goal, the quotas, and the working gift table. Ultimately, however, the working gift table, i.e., the table used throughout the campaign, will most likely become a self-fulfilled prophecy if it truly reflects the potential giving profile of the constituency.

7. (page 53) — Only the percentage changes. Today, annual giving campaigns more commonly target yearly increases of 10 per cent — about twice the recent rate of inflation.

8. (page 66) — In 1987, the American Cancer Society raised a total of $309,262,000 — over eight times the 1965 total.

9. (page 79) — The time period for conducting an annual campaign has extended considerably over the years. It is more common now for annual campaigns to be conducted year-round. Big capital campaigns now often run over seven years — up to 18 months of intense preparation, 60 months of campaign activity, and three to six months of

clean-up and celebration. The most common pledge-collection period is now five tax years rather than three.

In Mr. Seymour's time, fund-raising was generally thought of in terms of campaigns: the annual giving campaign, the capital campaign, etc. While this is still most often the case, there is also a trend now to view major-gift fund-raising as a continuing process — one that's not confined to a campaign period but one that's sustained throughout dips and peaks in highly visible campaign activity.

10. (page 84) — A system of combined telephone and mail solicitation is rapidly replacing the traditional direct mail approach to alumni solicitation. Telephone/mail can be used to solicit multi-year pledges. And the technique often significantly increases donor response, albeit at increased fund-raising cost. Indeed, more and more fund-raisers are using paid telephone solicitors, backed up by a series of supportive mailings, in the final phase of a capital campaign. Use of the telephone is clearly an extension of Mr. Seymour's emphasis upon personalization of the solicitation.

11. (page 89) — "Emerging organizations" — those without an established constituency or a record of successful fund-raising — are now expected to experience higher fund-raising costs than the estimates given by Mr. Seymour. For these organizations, a 30 per cent annual campaign cost and a 15 per cent capital campaign cost are considered reasonable ceilings.

12. (pages 91 & 176) — In 1987, the American Association of Fund-Raising Counsel had 33 member firms.

13. (page 91) — Today, of course, Mr. Seymour would add that both men and women now represent most fund-raising consulting firms.

14. (page 100) — The common practice now is to have a five-year pledge

period and, in special situations (e.g., extraordinarily large gifts), to extend that pledge period up to as much as 10 years.

15. (page 116) — Mr. Seymour's description of the development office mission will be challenged by some fund-raisers today as too narrow a definition. But actually, he probably defined the true basic role of the fund-raising executive in his time and ours quite correctly.

16. (page 123) — Currently, about 50 per cent of all fund-raising executives are women, and in higher education 17 per cent of the chief development officers are women.

17. (page 131) — Mr. Seymour's list of "special aspects of fund-raising" could now be expanded considerably. The recent evolution of philanthropy and fund-raising has brought us such things as the telephone/mail technique, computerized prospect screening, more sophisticated direct mail programs, the endowment campaign, the comprehensive campaign, employee deduction programs, multi-national campaigns, cause-related marketing, matching gift programs, grateful-patient solicitation, staff solicitation of big gifts, charity auctions, more intensive use of telethons and other television fund-raising techniques, affinity card campaigns, insurance/endowment campaigns, and celebrity-based one-time-event appeals that use national and international television and other media.

18. (page 140) — In 1987, 18 of the largest health agencies in the United States received a total of $1.187 billion.

19. (page 172) — Today, it is probably safe to say that a capital campaign of $500,000 or more dictates serious consideration of professional counsel. (Lesser goals challenge the cost-effectiveness of even the most

limited services by qualified outside counsel.) On the other hand, an annual campaign of $100,000 or more would probably justify limited use of counsel.

20. (page 177) — The code of the AAFRC was updated in 1987 to reflect social and technological changes. However, the basic principles and objectives of the original document were retained in the revision. Here is the current code.

Fair Practice Code: American Association of Fund-Raising Counsel, Inc. (AAFRC)

Guiding Principles. AAFRC member firms respect the American philanthropic tradition and the central role of men and women who founded our voluntary organizations, govern them, and are responsible for their financial support.

The member firms view the role of professional consultants in serving eleemosynary organizations as one of assisting and supporting the volunteers in their fund-raising responsibilities and strengthening their capabilities as leaders and solicitors.

Purpose. The purpose of the Code is to set forth fund-raising tenets, which member firms are expected to follow.

Membership. Firms that are exclusively or primarily organized to provide fund-raising counsel and direction are eligible for membership in the AAFRC. To qualify, firms must meet and maintain high standards of performance and demonstrate a record of success.

Service Provided. Member firms provide fund-raising counsel, conduct feasibility and planning studies, and offer campaign management, public relations and other related services.

Services are provided to 501(c)(3) organizations whose purposes and practices are deemed to be in the public interest.

Member firms do not engage in methods that are misleading to the public or harmful to their clients; do not make exaggerated claims of past achievement; and do not guarantee results or promise to help clients achieve unrealistic goals.

Payment of Services. Member firms believe it is in the best interest of clients that:

- fees be mututally agreed upon in advance and that they be based on the level and extent of services provided, except that initial meetings with prospective clients are not usually construed as services for which payment is expected;

- contracts providing for a contingent fee, commission or percentage of funds raised be avoided; and

- the services of professional solicitors who receive a contingent fee, commission or percentage of funds raised be avoided.

Further: Member firms also believe it is in the best interest of clients that solicitation of gifts should generally be undertaken by volunteers.

Member firms should not profit directly or indirectly from materials provided by others but billed through the member firms.

No payment should be made to an officer, director, trustee, employee or advisor of a nonprofit organization as compensation for influencing the selection of fund-raising counsel.

Any potential conflict of interest should be disclosed to clients and prospective clients.

21. (page 201) — The following list of recommended readings is merely a brief update to the literature that existed when Mr. Seymour drafted his "Recommended Readings" list.

For Better Background

The Art of Asking: How to Solicit Philanthropic Gifts, by Paul H. Schneiter, Fund-Raising Institute, Ambler, Pa., 1985.

This book focuses on the central act of fund-raising: the art of asking an individual for a gift in person. It's the type of solicitation that should be producing 80 per cent or more of most nonprofit causes' gift income.

The Art of Fund-Raising, by Irving R. Warner, Bantam Books, Inc., New York, revised 1984.

Centered on the participation of volunteers in the fund-raising process, this book provides practical advice and techniques for encouraging people to contribute.

The Complete Guide to Corporate Fund-Raising, edited by Joseph Dermer and Stephen Wertheimer, Public Service Materials Center, Washington, D.C., 1982.

The many aspects of corporate solicitation are described by some of the foremost American practitioners in the fund-raising field.

Dear Chris, Advice to a Volunteer Fund-Raiser, by John D. Verdery, The Taft Group, Inc., Washington, D.C., 1986.

This book is equally educational, personally satisfying, and encouraging for both the fund-raising volunteer and the professional. It represents a true insight into the fund-raising process.

Dear Friend: Masterminding the Art of Direct Mail Fund-Raising, by Kay Partney Lautman and Henry Goldstein, The Taft Group, Inc., Washington, D.C., 1984.

The most comprehensive book on direct mail available to both the novice and the professional. Must reading for anyone considering an aggressive and remunerative direct mail program.

The FRI Annual Giving Book, by M. Jane Williams, Fund-Raising Institute, Ambler, Pa., 1982.

Currently, the only comprehensive basic primer on how to start an annual giving program from scratch and to achieve its full potential. Contents range from staff and budgets to minimum gift clubs, challenge programs, and phonothons.

Fundraising in the United States: Its Role in America's Philanthropy, by Scott M. Cutlip, Rutgers University Press, New Brunswick, N.J., 1965.

To date, this publication is the only comprehensive history of American fund-raising.

Fund-Raising Research (a two-volume set), Fund-Raising Institute, Ambler, Pa., 1986.

Volume 1: How to Find Philanthropic Prospects, by Jeanne B. Jenkins and Marilyn Lucas, shows how to identify and evaluate prospective donors.

Volume 2: FRI Prospect-Research Resource Directory, issued every two or three years, is a comprehensive directory listing the resources — publications, databases, and services — that are the very basis of an effective prospect research program. It names and cross-indexes the resources and provides up to 13 key facts for each, including a detailed narrative description of contents.

Giving in America (Report of the Commission of Private Philanthropy and Public Needs), Washington, D.C., 1975.

A benchmark publication addressing the role of philanthropic giving in the United States, this report makes recommendations for Third Sector response to the need for increased giving.

Glossary of Fund-Raising Terms, National Society of Fund-Raising Executives Foundation, Alexandria, Va., 1986.

The most comprehensive compilation of definitions of commonly used fund-raising terms. Every fund-raising professional should be familiar with the terminology described in this publication.

The Golden Donors, by Waldemar A. Neilsen, Truman Talley Books/E.P. Dutton, New York, 1985.

An examination of the recent histories of America's 36 largest foundations. The author takes an often critical look at each foundation's programs and social impact.

How to Create and Use Solid Gold Fund-Raising Letters, by Arthur Lambert Cone Jr., Fund-Raising Institute, Ambler, Pa., 1987.

One of America's most successful appeal letter writers shares the insights of a long career. His book is easy to read and helpfully illustrated.

Major Challenges to Philanthropy, by Robert L. Payton, Independent Sector, Washington, D.C., 1984.

This publication is an examination of our society's principles of philanthropy. It challenges the very basis of the American philanthropic tradition in a non-threatening manner.

The Membership Mystique, by Richard P. Trenbeth, Fund-Raising Institute, Ambler, Pa., 1986.

The executive who pioneered in creating profitable membership programs for nonprofit groups teaches the reader how to launch and run a successful membership program — or to revitalize an existing program.

Philanthropy and Voluntarism: An Annotated Bibliography, by Daphne Niobe Layton, The Foundation Center, New York, 1987.

Some 1,614 books and articles are referenced in this work, which analyzes the historical, economic, journalistic, philosophical, statistical, sociological and other aspects of the philanthropic tradition in the United States and abroad.

Raising Funds From America's 2,000,000 Overlooked Corporations, by Aldo C. Podesta, Public Service Materials Center, Washington, D.C., 1984.

A practical guide to certain opportunities available to nonprofits through skilled utilization of corporate philanthropy.

Tested Ways to Successful Fund-Raising, by George A. Brakeley Jr., AMACOM, New York, 1980.

Detailed fundamentals of conducting a successful campaign are related to the basic aspects of the process and balanced against real experiences by one of the nation's leading fund-raising practitioners.

What Volunteers Should Know for Successful Fund-Raising, by Maurice G. Gurin, Stein and Day, New York, 1982.

A guide designed for volunteers engaged in big-gift fund-raising. It identifies for both volunteers and professionals the basic elements of fund-raising success.

22. (page 203) —*Giving USA* and its companion newsletter *Up-Date*, are now published by the American Association of Fund-Raising Counsel Trust for Philanthropy, 25 West 43rd Street, New York, NY 10036. *Giving USA*, an annual book, remains the definitive resource on American giving to philanthropic causes.

Philanthropic Digest is now published by Brakeley, John Price Jones Inc., 1600 Summer Street, Stamford, CT 06905. It is a periodical newsletter. Over the average year, it lists more than 6,000 current gifts, which usually have an aggregate total in excess of $2 billion. It is also available as "PD on Disk," a database version for the IBM/PC computer or compatible equipment.

Index

3137 028